creative ESSENTIALS

Patrick Nash

SHORT FILMS
writing the screenplay

creative ESSENTIALS

First published in 2012 by Kamera Books,
an imprint of Oldcastle Books
PO Box 394, Harpenden, Herts, AL5 1XJ
www.kamerabooks.com

Copyright © Patrick Nash 2012
Series Editor: Hannah Patterson

A CIP catalogue record for this book is available from the British Library.

978-1-84243-501-4 (Print)
978-1-84243-519-9 (epub)
978-1-84243-518-2 (kindle)
978-1-84243-520-5 (pdf)

25

Typeset by Elsa Mathern in Franklin Gothic 9 pt
Printed and Bound by Clays Ltd, Elcograf S.p.A.

CONTENTS

APPENDICES

INTRODUCTION

This book is designed to help short filmmakers understand the importance of finding and telling a great story, writing a properly constructed short screenplay and fully developing both it and the story it tells before shooting their film. It is also intended to help and encourage the many writers who fail to realise the benefits of writing short screenplays and jump prematurely straight into trying to write feature-length scripts. There is so much that a writer can learn by writing for short film. A beginning writer also stands a much better chance of having their work produced in this format. Few spec feature scripts are ever produced. Aspiring directors can also benefit by learning how to write and develop their story before filming. Sadly, too many skip this important stage to the detriment of their finished film.

Short film is an excellent training ground for writers and filmmakers alike. It's a place where you can experiment, develop and learn, make mistakes, acquire a broad range of filmmaking skills, meet other writers and filmmakers and perfect your craft before trying to join the mainstream. Writing and directing short films is a great way to demonstrate your talent and ability to the industry as a whole. It also allows you to gain recognition by winning awards at film festivals and in industry-related screenplay competitions. Your work will be your calling card. It will help you to break into one of the most competitive industries on Earth.

Short film introduces aspiring filmmakers to the process of filmmaking. It's where many directors, actors, technical crew and writers serve their apprenticeship. Many successful short filmmakers have gone on to direct feature films. Fifty-one of the 105 directors nominated for the Best Director Oscar since 1990 began their careers making short films. This book is intended to help writers and directors write professional short-film screenplays and to avoid the many pitfalls I've observed as a member of a short-film selection panel and jury at an Oscar-accredited film festival.

There has been an explosion in short filmmaking in recent years, stimulated by the technological revolution in relatively low-cost, high-quality filmmaking equipment, by the rapid expansion in the number of film festivals and film schools worldwide and the rapid growth of cyberspace. The Internet and sites such as YouTube, Vimeo, MySpace, Facebook and indeed the countless number of personalised websites provide filmmakers with unlimited opportunities to distribute, screen and promote their work internationally.

The scale of access and opportunity is unprecedented in the history of short film. However, I believe the general public does not really appreciate short film as an entertainment and storytelling medium. There are many excellent short films out there but, alas, there are an even greater number that are not. Why do they fail? The biggest cause of failure in short filmmaking today is the absence of an interesting and emotionally engaging story, and that, I believe, is why many people are reluctant to watch them. Ultimately, story is what audiences want to see and story is what wins filmmakers the awards and accolades. Screenwriters and filmmakers are storytellers and story is king. If you want to be successful, you must find a way to tell winning stories.

LESSONS FROM THE FOYLE FILM FESTIVAL

This book came about as a result of my involvement in, and membership of, the short-film selection panel and juries at the Oscar-accredited Foyle Film Festival in my hometown of Derry City in Northern Ireland. I've also been a filmmaker with the local film centre, the Nerve Centre, and have written many short and several feature-length screenplays. For many years the Foyle Film Festival was the only Oscar-accredited film festival in Britain and Ireland. The Encounters International Film Festival in Bristol has recently joined it. The only other way of qualifying for Oscar consideration in Britain is by winning at BAFTA. The full list of accredited and qualifying festivals can be found on the Academy Awards website under Rule 19.

Winning the award for best film in the International Short, Irish Short or Animation category at Foyle automatically makes your film eligible for Oscar consideration and a number of winners have gone on to be nominated and win over the years. This book includes the screenplays from two of the most recently nominated short films – Juanita Wilson's *The Door* and Michael Creagh's *The Crush*.

I have to admit I love short films and must have watched thousands over the years. I love it when we get together on selection days with our box of discs. It's like Christmas. Typically we'll watch maybe 40 or 50 films in a single day. We'll spend many days doing this in the run up to the film festival in November. It's always exciting seeing the box of discs arrive and then dipping into it at random, not knowing what each screening will bring. Every day we find gems but, alas, we also find far too many that fail for a variety of avoidable reasons.

THE NEED FOR STORY

In 2009 I decided to keep a notebook and list all the various mistakes, failings and issues we noticed as we watched. I ended up with a list of over 70 points but three things in particular stood out. Bad acting, bad sound and, most of all, the failure to tell an interesting and involving story. Poor storytelling was the number one reason why films failed. They either lacked a story altogether or the story was boring, uninspiring and underdeveloped. Sometimes there was a good idea at the heart of the film but the filmmaker had failed to make the best use of it. It also appeared that a significant number of the films lacked the involvement of an experienced or trained writer.

It makes me sad to see the amount of effort filmmakers have clearly put into their films, and I know how difficult it can be, without getting this important step right. If you want to be successful, you must find a great story to tell. You must write a proper screenplay and develop it to the full BEFORE you start shooting your film. If you do not, your film will most likely be stillborn and all your effort will have been wasted. I can't emphasise this enough. It is the number-one lesson and reason for writing this book. Find a great story and write a great screenplay. Don't cut corners.

Ultimately, if you want to make it as a professional in this business, as I'm sure many of the readers do, then work like one, adopt professional work methods and learn how to tell a story. Audiences love story and great storytelling is what wins the awards. Excite, entertain and enthral them. Stir their hearts and passions. Give them a powerful emotional experience. My main focus in this book will be on dramatic storytelling as that is where I believe the core of a writer's and filmmaker's business lies.

TWELVEPOINT.COM

This book began life in those selection-day notes and a discussion about writing for short film on the writer's forum on the Twelvepoint.com website in early 2010. As a result of that discussion I eventually wrote 15 articles on various aspects of short filmmaking for the website. This in turn led, by way of the London Screenwriters Festival and a discussion with my agent, Julian Friedmann of Blake Friedmann Literary Agency, to the current book. I'd like to thank Julian and Hannah Patterson of Kamera Books for all their help and assistance in making this book possible and also to Jonquil Florentin who edited and prepared my original 15 articles for publication on the Twelvepoint website. I'd also like to thank the Foyle Film Festival director, Bernie

McLaughlin, and all the staff of the Foyle Film Festival and the Nerve Centre in Derry for all their years of work and for giving me the opportunity to assist and participate. It's been an invaluable source of knowledge and experience.

In this book I will focus in particular on the need to find and tell a great story. I will explain what a short screenplay is and what the benefits are for the writer in writing one. I will discuss proper format, structure, length and how to find ideas. I will look at the key features of a screenplay and look at some of the dos and don'ts of writing a story for screen. I will look at character, dialogue and conflict, how to begin and end your screenplay, motivation and goals, twists and hooks, and focus especially on the need to give the audience an emotional experience. I will discuss the need to write loglines, treatments and synopses and the need to rewrite. I will discuss the various problems that can occur and also examine short screenplay competitions.

I will finish with three examples of short-film screenplays including those for two Oscar-nominated films, *The Door* and *The Crush*. I'd also like to thank Juanita Wilson and Octagon Films for allowing me to reproduce the screenplay for the former film in this book and taking the time to talk to me about the writing and making of this excellent short film. I'd also like to thank Michael Creagh and Purdy Pictures for giving me permission to include his winning screenplay for *The Crush* and again also taking the time to speak to me about writing and making the film. I hope you enjoy the book and I hope that it'll help you write an award-winning script of your own and launch your filmmaking career.

Patrick Nash

1. A SHORT HISTORY

SHORT AND SILENT

Once upon a time, all film was short... and silent. The earliest films were little, one- or two-minute 'actualities' that showed single shots of everyday scenes such as trains arriving in stations, workers leaving factories, street scenes and so on. These moving images fascinated early audiences but the novelty soon wore off. Audiences wanted more, so filmmakers began to produce longer pieces showing popular vaudeville acts, slapstick-comedy routines, dancing girls, exotic locations and even short narrative stories such as Georges Méliès' *A Trip to the Moon* (1902) and Edwin S Porter's *The Great Train Robbery* (1903).

With the rapid development in film stock, camera and projection equipment and basic film grammar in both Europe and America, filmmaking became more ambitious. Films now began to tell longer, more complex stories. However, as this was the Silent Era, the visuals had to do all the work – there was no dialogue. Early screenwriters – who were known as scenario writers – began to emerge, typically from theatrical backgrounds. Their job was to create short narrative stories – scenarios – that could be told using simple visual images. They drew heavily on plays and novels for inspiration. The need to communicate also led to the exaggerated gestures, facial expressions and theatricality of the actors that became so characteristic of this era. Slapstick comedy was particularly popular because of its highly visual style.

By 1910, it's estimated that there were over 10,000 Nickelodeons in the USA alone. One- and two-reel films of 10 to 20 minutes' duration were the most common type of product screened by them. At that time the standard reel of black-and-white film stock was 900 to 1,000 feet long and ran for between 10 and 12 minutes of screen time.

THE BIRTH OF THE FEATURE... AND 'SHORT' FILM

More ambitious film directors like DW Griffith soon realised they could tell longer stories simply by adding more reels. 'Multi-reelers', as they were initially called, appeared as early as 1906 with the world's first officially recorded feature film being John Tait's Australian-made *The True Story of the Kelly Gang*. Others followed in the USA, Britain, Italy, France, Germany, Denmark and Eastern Europe, with some, like Italy's 1914 historical spectacular *Cabiria*, being up to twelve reels long. However, one- and two-reelers remained the norm.

It wasn't until 1915 that a feature film appeared that changed the filmmaking landscape forever. DW Griffith's highly controversial three-hour Ku Klux Klan epic *The Birth of a Nation* brought together all that was then known of filmmaking and storytelling technique and blew audiences away. It was a sensation in spite of its blatant racism and made a fortune at the box office. It took filmmaking to a whole new level. Suddenly, audiences and producers alike wanted to see and make long films that told more complex, sophisticated and emotionally involving stories. The studios began to churn them out by the hundred with many being tailor-made vehicles for the rising stars of the new Hollywood star system.

One- and two-reelers continued to remain immensely popular but they were now relegated to the role of support act to the main attraction or main 'feature' as it was known. They came to be known as 'short films' or 'short subjects' as opposed to the longer 'feature films', and so the term 'short film' was born. The most popular shorts were slapstick comedies by the likes of Charlie Chaplin, Buster Keaton, Harold Lloyd and the Keystone Cops, westerns and serials such as *The Perils Of Pauline* and newsreels such as *Pathé News* and *Movietone*.

A PACKAGE DEAL

Going to the 'Moving Picture Palace' was a big deal at that time, a social event, and theatre owners soon realised that, as well as the ticket prices, they could make as much, if not more, on the confections, drinks, popcorn, or whatever else they sold the audiences. The longer they could keep the audience captive in the theatre, the more they were likely to spend and consume. Hence, a shorts programme would accompany every feature with each film separated by an intermission – ostensibly to allow the projectionist to change reels but also to allow the patrons time to buy refreshments. Singers and stage musicians often accompanied these shorts packages as well. Shorts filled a useful commercial niche and were used to warm up audiences and fill theatre time. Some of the most popular even grew to half an hour in length or were serialised, e.g. Laurel & Hardy in the 'thirties.

The studios found that making shorts was a useful way to maximise the use of their expensive real estate, filmmaking resources and contract employees. Everyone was on fixed contracts and pay in those days, and shorts kept them busy when they weren't making features. The studios used their control of the theatre chains and block booking to ensure that everything they made was exhibited commercially. Animated shorts – or cartoons, as they came to be known – became very popular in the late 1920s. Walt Disney built a whole studio system around them. The studios recognised that making shorts was a useful way to train and test their production staff, upcoming actors and directors. Some independent production companies specialised in making shorts, which they later sold or rented to the studios and movie-theatre chains.

THE RISE OF THE 'B' MOVIE

By the early 1930s, the standard movie programme included live performers, a newsreel, a short or serial, a cartoon and a feature film. However, following the introduction of sound in 1927 and the appearance of colour film, this began to change as the B movie appeared. The B movie was a long film that supported the main feature but was not quite as long and generally not of the same standard. It's suggested that the name came from the studios referring to their short-film production units as 'B units' – facilities that they turned over en masse to making these low-budget support features.

B movies appeared in rapidly increasing numbers throughout the 1930s and 1940s and sounded the death knell for commercially produced studio shorts. Despite the appearance of musical shorts from 1927 to 1933, the studios soon stopped making shorts altogether to concentrate all their resources on making features. Live performers and shorts gradually disappeared, as 'double bills' became the norm. Newsreels were retained as a public service and were of particular importance during the war years but they couldn't compete with the arrival of television news in the 1950s.

With the death of the studio system in the early 1950s, the end of block booking and the rise of television across the developed world, shorts all but disappeared. It was cheaper for owners of movie theatres or cinemas – as they became known outside North America – to programme a 'double bill'. The short format was now more suited to television where the half-hour slot became a standard programming unit. Half-hour episodes of favourite programmes, soap operas, cartoons, serials and comedy shows like *The Lucy Show* punctuated by adverts became the norm. Soon, the most common type of short film to be found globally was the television commercial.

ARTHOUSE AND ENTHUSIASTIC AMATEURS

For a time after the war, independently produced shorts were only made by enthusiastic or wealthy amateurs in film clubs, the few film schools then in existence, or by organisations such as the information units of Government Departments. There were few outlets for exhibiting them outside the arthouse circuit. Film festivals were still few in number and tended to focus on celebrity directors, feature films and stars. Studios no longer needed shorts to train and test their employees – they could do that making B movies. Those who entered broadcasting found that the networks had their own programming requirements and restrictions, with little room for independently minded short filmmakers who wanted to do their own thing.

Furthermore, without the help of production companies and studios, making a short film was not an easy thing to do. Film stock and equipment were neither cheap nor plentiful and processing and editing a film was expensive. In the 'fifties and 'sixties portable 16mm cameras designed for newsgathering during World War Two did become available together with lightweight Super 8mm cartridge-loaded cameras designed for the amateur home-movie market. After World War Two many second-hand 16mm cameras found their way into the hands of aspiring directors and short filmmakers in Europe and America. The French New Wave and Italian Neo-Realists made use of them. Independently made shorts were produced in small numbers but the quality was sometimes poor due to the filmmaker's lack of resources and experience.

FILM SCHOOLS AND TECHNOLOGY

In the 1960s a number of significant film schools such as those at NYU, CalArts, Columbia and UCLA were founded in the USA. Short filmmaking became a standard training and graduation vehicle. Graduates, including such famous names as Scorsese, Lucas and

Coppola, made short films to showcase their talent. Since then there has been a steady increase in the number of film schools established around the world. The pace accelerated dramatically in the 1980s and 1990s as a result of the technological revolution in high-quality, low-cost camera technology.

First, in the 1980s, lightweight video cameras appeared that recorded analog video direct to tape. This was followed in the mid 1990s by more sophisticated digital camcorders recording high-quality video digitally on tape with Mini-DV being the most popular format. Hard discs, DVDs, mini discs and, more recently, solid-state memory cards have replaced tape as the storage media of choice. This ability to film on a low budget was complemented by the ability to edit on a home computer or laptop using editing software such as Final Cut Pro.

This revolution in filmmaking technology and the dramatic reduction in cost, together with the ever-increasing availability of equipment, brought about a renaissance in short filmmaking. Short films are being made on everything from mobile phones to sophisticated prosumer cameras. With almost every family having a camcorder for home movies, the public are much more camera literate. The level of interest in filmmaking has increased exponentially and brought with it an explosion in short filmmaking.

Most countries now have universities with dedicated film departments. Specialist film schools and centres have sprung up in many major cities. Public funding alone accounts for more than 1,000 short films per annum in Europe, not counting those produced in film schools. The UKFC estimated in October 2009 that 2,000 short films had been produced the previous year in the UK with 1,800 through the various film schools and departments of higher education, 150 through public funding and a further 50 privately funded by independent filmmakers. Furthermore, this doesn't count the vast quantity of user-generated content uploaded to sites like YouTube.

FESTIVALS AND THE INTERNET

Hand in hand with this explosion of interest in filmmaking there's been an upsurge in the number of film festivals established worldwide offering outlets for short film. Online submission manager, Withoutabox, now lists over 3,000 festivals worldwide with around 1,000 of these hosting short-film programmes, competitions and awards. Some, like Clermont-Ferrand or Tampere, specialise entirely in short film... and then there is the Internet.

The arrival of the Internet presented short filmmakers with a screening outlet unlike any other in history. Films can be uploaded to sites such as YouTube and made instantly available to a global audience. Short films can be viewed on everything from Internet cable channels to personal, specialist or organisational websites, social-networking sites, mobile phones and pay-per-view or video-on-demand sites. Individual short films even have their own websites and Facebook pages charting their progress from pre-production to winning awards. The Internet, electronic-communications media and the proliferation of film festivals have given short filmmakers opportunities for exhibition and promotion unheard of since the early days of film, while the technological revolution has given them the means to realise their dreams, producing high-quality films on relatively low budgets.

But while short filmmaking has returned on a scale unseen since the early days of cinema, something is still missing. Despite the technology, training and opportunities, many films are still poor. As a member of the short-film selection panel at the Foyle Film Festival, I see far too many short films that fail because of bad acting, poor sound recording, lighting issues, but most of all because of an underdeveloped, poorly crafted or uninspiring story. Indeed, some lack a story altogether. All short films need to begin with a great idea and a well-written and carefully crafted screenplay. Too many short filmmakers skip this vital step in their rush to become directors.

Instead of finding a good writer and screenplay, many try to write it themselves with little or no screenwriting ability whatsoever. Short films need good writers and screenplays, but what's in it for the writer? Why should he or she write a short screenplay?

2. WHY WRITE SHORT SCREENPLAYS?

Why write a short screenplay? What's in it for the writer? Indeed, what kind of short screenplays are we talking about? This question can be answered in several ways, but as this book is about short-screenplay writing this chapter will mainly focus on the writer's point of view. First, it's necessary to elaborate on the type of short films and filmmakers we're talking about.

WHO MAKES SHORT FILMS TODAY?

In my opinion – and these are generalisations – short filmmakers today can be divided into three broad groups:

1. **The 'high end' professional short filmmakers** who work on commercials, promos, music videos, travelogues, corporate and informational films and other professionally commissioned shorts.

2. **The amateur, recreational and fun filmmakers** – the average members of the public who upload a huge volume of self-produced content to YouTube, Facebook and other social-networking and Internet sites.

3. **The beginning, aspiring or emerging filmmakers** who wish to develop a professional career within the film or television

industry or those already part way there. This group usually
has a particular interest in writing, directing and working in
fictional drama.

The first group, the professionals, are already well established in the
business and make their short films through established production
companies with access to professional crews, high-quality equipment
and substantial budgets. Some work for companies who have long-
standing client relationships with the organisations that commission
this type of material. The end product is usually very polished and
professional. Such experienced professionals are often contracted to
work as freelances on television and film projects.

However, writers have limited scope for original screenplay work
within this sector. Typically, the filmmaker must work to a tightly
defined brief from the customer whether it's an advertising agency,
business organisation, government department or music company.
The brief, product, artist, music lyrics or sponsor's message very much
dictate the script that will be written and used. Elaborate storyboards
and shot lists often replace scripts in this area. Occasionally, there will
be some small narrative element to the project.

The second group, the amateur, recreational or family filmmakers,
usually lack filmmaking technique and have no desire to enter the film
industry. They are simply having fun with their camcorder and posting
a huge volume of very diverse material on to the Internet. Much of
the material is simply observational footage captured by chance. It
ranges from kids and animals doing funny things to coverage of public
events, dramatic 'on-the-spot' footage of newsworthy incidents, short
performance or instructional videos and unusual tourist videos or
holiday shots – *The Battle of Kruger* is a must see. The key factor
in all this material is that little, if any, of it has been professionally
scripted or produced.

Finally, to the third group, the aspiring or emerging professionals,
those who wish to break into the mainstream and develop long-term

careers in the film and television industry. This group, to which I believe most of the readers of this book belong, wish to earn a living writing, directing and telling fictional or, indeed, true stories in visual form. It's a career choice as well as a personal passion. This group is driven by a creative desire and ambition to bring dramatic, exciting and emotionally stirring stories to life on screen while making a living doing what they enjoy most.

The biggest problem facing this group is how to get noticed, how to demonstrate their talent and ability to the industry, win commissions and break into the mainstream. This is where short films and short screenplays come in. This book and the advice it gives is primarily intended to meet the needs of this third group of filmmakers and the type of short films they most want to produce – drama in all its many shapes and forms.

THE ROLE OF SHORT FILM

Short films, as well as being an art form in their own right, have three main roles for filmmakers:

1. A calling card

2. A training ground

3. A means to acquire credits, awards and recognition

Short films are used as a calling card to demonstrate the talent and ability of the filmmaker to the industry. In effect, the film and screenplay says, 'This is me and this is what I can do.' Generally, though, short film is seen as a director's medium with the director and principal actors gaining the majority of the attention. However, the writer will also benefit if the film he or she scripts wins a major award at, for example, BAFTA, the Oscars, Cannes, Berlin, Venice or Sundance, if he or she is the writer-director, or if the screenplay wins a major award at a high-profile screenplay contest. Implicit in this concept of the short as a calling card is the idea of quality and excellence. If you want to showcase your talent, your work needs to be the very best you can offer.

Short films are an invaluable training ground and a place for talent development. They are an apprenticeship, a place where you can learn the craft of screenwriting and filmmaking 'on the job'. It's a place to experiment creatively, acquire experience, test techniques and become proficient in the use of every filmmaking tool. They give writers and filmmakers the opportunity to network and develop contacts, especially at festivals where they can meet other filmmakers, writers, producers and potential collaborators.

Finally, short filmmaking is a means to acquire credits and recognition through public screenings, winning competitions at festivals and high-profile screenplay competitions or winning awards such as the Oscar or BAFTA. Credits from the most high-profile festivals draw substantial attention to the talent and ability of the filmmaker and significantly improve their chances of securing future commissions, work and funding. Many award-winning short filmmakers have gone on to write and direct feature films.

Many in today's film industry learned their trade in shorts. As I said in the introduction to this book, 51 of the 105 nominees for Best Director at the Oscars from 1990 to 2010 began their careers making short films, including 11 of the 21 winners. These 11 winners included Steven Soderbergh, Roman Polanski, Steven Spielberg, Robert Zemeckis, James Cameron, Ron Howard, Peter Jackson, Martin Scorsese, Kathryn Bigelow and Tom Hooper. Some professionals still give freely of their time, sharing their knowledge and experience and helping to train the filmmakers of tomorrow by helping them to make their shorts.

WHAT'S IN IT FOR THE WRITER?

I've already mentioned that generally it's the director or principal actors who get the most attention from making short films, so what's in it for the writer? Why should he or she bother to join the process and write a short screenplay? Let's look at the many good reasons.

Transferable Skills – All the skills you learn and use writing short screenplays are transferable to the process of writing feature films and television drama. Short screenplays will teach you economy, how to tell a powerful story using strong imagery and the minimum of words. This discipline will prove invaluable later in your career.

Training – The opportunity to learn, develop and refine your writing skills and master screenwriting technique with the possibility of quickly seeing the end result on screen.

Growth – The chance as a beginner to make mistakes and learn and grow in a safe or less punishing environment.

Experience – Writing short screenplays will help you to accumulate writing experience, especially if you write across a range of genres and lengths. The subject matter also ranges wider than most feature films. Risks can be taken and creativity let fly in ways that are unusual in mainstream film and television drama. You can stretch your writing muscle by exploring unusual scenarios in new and imaginative ways.

Testing Ideas – Short screenplays can be used to test ideas, concepts and characters for larger projects. For example, Neil Blomkamp's highly successful 2009 science fiction feature film *District 9* grew out of his six-minute 2005 short film *Alive In Joburg*. The 112-minute-long film was shot in South Africa for $30 million and nominated for no less than four Academy Awards including Best Picture. A writer should always be alive to the possibility that what he's writing as a short may contain the seeds of a feature as well.

Awards and Credits – Writing short screenplays presents you with the opportunity to enter short-screenplay competitions and win awards. It permits you to market test your script against hundreds of others, while winning major awards builds industry recognition and your credibility as a writer. It demonstrates your writing ability and talent and can attract interest and even business from producers and commissioners. Similarly, if your short film is actually produced and entered into prominent festivals, further success can follow. Major awards can kick-start careers.

Exposure – Writing a short screenplay and having it produced provides you with the chance to showcase your work, market yourself, demonstrate your ability and receive valuable feedback from script readers, fellow writers, audiences or industry professionals.

Performance Material – Short screenplays provide ideal material for use in writers' and actors' groups, e.g. for table reads and stand-up performances. Many writers join writers groups so they can test material, receive feedback, socialise and collaborate with like-minded individuals. Some theatres and drama groups periodically offer writers the opportunity to test scenes or script excerpts using trained actors. Listening to an enthusiastic table read or watching actors perform your work for the first time is an experience few writers ever forget. Seeing your characters come to life in the mouths of actors will give your confidence and self-belief an enormous boost.

Portfolio – Writing short screenplays will help you to build a portfolio of work that demonstrates what you can do across a range of genres, styles and lengths. It provides you with samples of work to show potential partners, agents and commissioning editors. It shows that you can write and are not a one-trick pony. It can help you find your 'voice' and discover what you're best at.

Achievement – Completing a short screenplay gives you, the writer, a sense of achievement – you've actually completed a script that works. It's easier to finish a 15-minute screenplay than a 90-minute feature script. Completion builds confidence in your ability, especially if the script later becomes a short film. Confidence motivates and drives success. Many a writer has started a feature script only to give up half way through because the effort required was just too great for them at that point in time. Completing a good short script proves that you can do it, gives you a sense of accomplishment and increases the chance that you will finish longer works.

Production – You have a better chance of having your work produced independently with a well-written short screenplay than with a feature screenplay. The budget and effort required pose less of an obstacle.

DIY Filmmaking – Completing a short script and seeing it turned into a short film can open the door to other possibilities and encourage you to do it yourself. It gives you the chance to become a hyphenate: a writer-director. Writer-directors have greater clout and credibility within the industry. Making a short film based on your own screenplay can act as the entry point to micro-budget and low-budget feature filmmaking. Many short filmmakers and writers have travelled this road with success.

Production experience – Short-film writers who have their short screenplays produced frequently participate in the making of their own film. It's the perfect opportunity to experience a film set and learn the roles, skills and reality of filmmaking. You'll learn what it's like to work as part of a production team with real actors, crew... and problems. It is an invaluable way to learn how a screenplay is turned into a film and how it has to be rewritten and adapted to meet the needs, practicalities and constraints of filmmaking. It's a lesson that will serve you well when you come to write your next screenplay.

The stepping-stones approach – If you can write a 15-minute screenplay, there's no reason why you couldn't do a 30-minute one, while 30 minutes could lead to 45- or 60-minute pieces. If you can master a one-hour piece, there's little reason why you couldn't manage a 90-minute feature. In effect, you start small and work your way up the ladder of creativity and success while adapting your writing technique to the needs of the different lengths and formats. You have to walk before you can run and short films are the perfect place for new writers to start.

The Messenger – You write because you have a message to sell. You want to write about something you are passionate about and stir the viewer to action. You have a message to communicate about something that is important to you. You want to enlighten, inspire, convey meaning and draw attention to some issue you feel deeply about. If so, you need to be subtle and not lecture or hector as if on a soapbox. Audiences do not like being preached to. The most effective method is to raise the issue as a question that provokes thought through a powerful, deeply emotional story.

The Showman – You write for the pleasure of entertaining the crowd and hearing their applause. Performing to an audience and hearing the 'roar of the crowd' are powerful motivators in their own right in the entertainment industry.

So you can see there are many good reasons and a lot of benefits for a writer writing short screenplays. In the short term, you may not make much money from it – few do in short film – but you're laying a strong foundation for your future career and learning lessons and skills that will prove invaluable down the line. So what is a screenplay? A blueprint or an emotional experience written down on paper?

3. WHAT IS A SHORT SCREENPLAY?

It's essential to understand what a screenplay is and what its role or purpose is before you begin to write. What are its essential components? The 'short' part is easy to explain – officially, it's anything that is shorter than 40 minutes of screen time or 40 pages of standard-format screenplay. Of course, in reality, they're usually substantially shorter than that but more of that in the next chapter. So, what is a screenplay?

On the one hand, it can be argued that a short screenplay is a story, an emotional experience or perhaps even a message or lesson in life written down on paper. On the other, as regards the mechanics of screenwriting and the process of filmmaking, the screenplay is best regarded as a blueprint, a very particular type of blueprint.

A BLUEPRINT

The architect's blueprint is the most popular analogy used to explain what a screenplay is. An architect's blueprint is a plan for the construction of a building. It describes all the elements necessary to construct that building and is written in a way that construction engineers the world over can understand. It lays out the basic structure but does not go into fine detail on décor, furnishings and so on. It leaves that to others. The blueprint is a practical working document that will only be seen by construction experts. The end user sees only the finished building.

Similarly, a screenplay is a blueprint or plan for a film that contains all the elements necessary to enable a team of filmmakers to construct a story visually on screen. It is written in a very specific way following certain rules and conventions of format, structure and layout, which we will discuss later. It adheres to screenwriting rules that have been learned over a century of filmmaking. Everyone who works professionally in the film industry understands this universal language. It simplifies the process of turning a written story into a film.

Like the architect's blueprint it does not go into fine detail, leaving that to experts like set designers, location managers, the art department, sound designers and so on. For example, if a scene is set in the intensive-care unit of a hospital, it's not necessary for the screenwriter to describe it in detail in the way that say a novelist would. It is sufficient to say INT – INTENSIVE CARE UNIT – DAY in the scene heading and the art department, location managers, set designers and costume department will take over. They will find a real hospital ICU that can be used, or research and build one in a studio if that proves to be more cost effective. That's their job. The screenwriter is left free to concentrate on telling the story, what actually happens in that unit.

The screenplay tells the story. It acts as a point of reference for the cast and crew and allows pre-production to plan and schedule the shoot. It acts as a visual guide as well as a blueprint and gives the story its spine or structure. Like a musical score, it is a unique literary form that is specially designed for a specific purpose – making a film. It's simple, sparse, full of technical abbreviations and structured in a way that tells each of the different film departments what they need to know in order to make that film.

Screenwriting is not literature, poetry or prose. Unlike these literary forms, the end user – the audience – never sees a screenplay. It's a practical working document, a means to an end, with the final product being a completed film telling a story in pictures live on screen. Unfortunately, this relationship to literature often leads to some members of the artistic community looking down on screenwriting as a lesser form. On the other hand, few great novelists have ever been able to adapt to the sparseness and peculiar storytelling technicalities of screenwriting. The two forms are quite different but equally challenging to do well.

THE KEY COMPONENTS

There are five key components to every screenplay, whether short or long:

1. Scenes

2. Characters

3. Action or Description

4. Dialogue

5. Parentheticals

These are the basic building blocks of the screenplay. You, as the writer, must tell your story using each of these elements. It's important to note that, while scenes are the most visible structural component in the screenplay, film traditionally has four main components:

1. **Three Acts** – a beginning, middle and end

2. **Sequences** – a collection of scenes telling a self-contained part of the story

3. **Scenes** – each composed of a series of shots or story beats

4. **Shots** – the basic unit of film and the basic editing component

While only scenes are formally written down in the screenplay, it's important that every writer appreciates the relevance of the other three components to his or her story. Story beats are the nearest writing equivalent to shots. They are the little action-reaction moments that go to build a scene. Shots are the director's nearest visual equivalent. Feature films are not the only films with these components. Short films, which tell a dramatic story, also have a beginning, middle and end and may even contain mini-sequences depending on the length and complexity of the story. Indeed, it's often argued that narrative short films closely resemble sequences in feature-length films.

Every feature film can be broken down into sequences, each of which tells a self-contained part of the main story. For example, in the film *Gladiator*, the opening battle in Germania, which introduces Maximus, is a sequence; Proximo's gladiator school is a sequence; the epic gladiator battle in the arena, which ends with Maximus revealing his true identity, is a sequence; and so on. As well as being part of the larger whole, each sequence tells its own story. Every sequence will have its own beginning, middle and end and run for up to 15 minutes or more. The similarity with narrative short films is therefore obvious.

Finally, every scene will be constructed from a series of shots carefully selected and edited to tell that little part of the story. It is the director's job to decide how the scene will be shot, not the writer's. The director, with the help of a storyboard, shot list and the cinematographer will work out the various shots required to capture the essence of the scene, then later, in postproduction, will decide with the editor how each shot is cut together to best tell the story visually. It's important that the writer understands this process and how the various parts of the screenplay must fit together to tell the story. Acts, sequences and shots will be present and understood in the story but will not be formally written down. They are an essential part of the filmmaking and storytelling process.

SHOW, DON'T TELL

'Show, don't tell' is a piece of screenwriting advice that is so widely used it has almost become a cliché. Filmmaking is a visual business and a screenplay is a visual document. You must tell your story using only what can be shown on screen. It must be active, exciting, emotionally involving. Don't have your characters tell each other the story, have them show us the story by their actions, by what they do, the decisions they make, the things they say or don't say, and so on.

Your screenplay should enable those who read it to 'see' the story. There must be no long flowery prose or long-winded description. Adjectives and adverbs should be used sparingly. A screenwriter must have a mind's 'eye' for the visual. He must think in pictures, write in pictures and use vivid imagery.

Nothing should be included in a screenplay that cannot be shown on screen. For example, in a novel it's possible to describe what a character thinks, but how do you do this on screen? Sometimes voiceovers are used; for example, Martin Sheen's voiceovers in *Apocalypse Now* or Kevin Spacey's in *American Beauty*, but doing this too much can become tiresome for audiences. It is, however, an accepted storytelling style in film noir. Some screenplays have characters writing their thoughts down in diaries or logs but again this should only be used sparingly. It's regarded as lazy storytelling. Generally, characters must show us what they think by what they do, how they react to problems, make decisions and respond to others. Part of the fun of watching a movie is trying to figure out what a character really thinks.

WRITE IN THE PRESENT

Screenplays are ALWAYS written in the PRESENT TENSE. This is a crucial rule of screenwriting. The viewer and, indeed, reader must feel that they are watching the story unfold in real time. It must feel immediate, vivid and exciting, as if they're actively present in the scene and don't know what's going to happen next. No matter what era the story is set in, or whether it's a flashback or dream, everything you see must be written in the present tense.

Stories unfold on screen in real time, or so it seems. Screen time is always 'the present'. This is key to audience engagement and emotional involvement. Psychologically, it allows the viewer to invest emotionally in the characters and buy into the story and their predicament. It makes it 'feel' real and therefore all the more exciting.

Always use active verbs and avoid adverbs – verbal adjectives. Avoid passive expressions, words ending with '–ing' and phrases such as 'starts to' or 'begins to'. For example:

- Walks slowly – strolls

- Runs quickly – dashes, darts, sprints

- Is walking – walks

- Starts to eat – eats

- Begins to dig – digs

Using active verbs and eliminating adverbs will vastly improve the pace of the read. It makes scenes appear more immediate and dramatic. Make it active, simple and clear to read. Avoid unnecessary adjectives and choose the ones you do use wisely. Keep sentences short and avoid long, convoluted sentences full of punctuation. Grammar and sentence structure, which are perfectly fine in prose, can be cumbersome and slow to read in a screenplay. You should aim to make your script fast, active, vivid and visual. Use evocative words and strong visual imagery. Buy a good thesaurus and dictionary and use them.

WRITERS' DRAFTS AND SHOOTING SCRIPTS

There are two types of screenplays – writers' drafts and shooting scripts. The writer always writes what is known as the writer's draft. This screenplay concentrates on telling the visual story and, at feature-film level, is usually read by a producer, development executive, commissioning editor and director. If purchased by a production company it will go into development, aka development hell, where it will be rewritten many times. Once everyone is happy with the result the screenplay will be 'locked', the project will be 'greenlit' and put into pre-production. The writer NEVER writes camera directions, scene numbers, editing and technical directions in his screenplay.

Once the script goes into pre-production it becomes a shooting script. Every scene will be numbered and the director will add camera angles together with cues for special effects, stunts, sound effects and so on. Each department uses this new version of the script to plan, budget and schedule production. Shooting scripts are the most common type of script to be found on the Internet or in print, together with unofficial and incorrectly formatted transcripts. They are not writer's drafts and can mislead aspiring writers. Study and learn from the original writer's drafts if you can locate them.

Of course, this distinction can be blurred in the short-film world where the writer may also be the director and short screenplays are seldom sold to production companies. However, if you wish to become a professional writer, begin as you mean to continue. Be professional from the outset. If you submit your short screenplay to a screenplay contest or to a film organisation for funding, they will expect to see a properly formatted writer's draft.

So now you know what a short screenplay is, let's look at structure and length.

4. STRUCTURE AND LENGTH

STRUCTURE

It's often said that anything goes with short films and that filmmakers can use any structure they please to tell their story. While short film does indeed offer that degree of creative freedom, it's also true that structure is extremely important to effective storytelling. Structure is the dramatic organisation of all the elements that go together to make up your film. It's the framework that underpins the story and fits everything together. Where story is the 'what', structure is the 'how'. Finding the right structure for your story can make or break it. In my experience, watching countless short films during selection days at the Foyle Film Festival, and thousands more online, there are three broad types of structure to be found in short films today.

1. The 'Joke' Structure

2. The Traditional Three-Act Structure

3. The Experimental

Each of these has consequences for the length and content of the short film and its chances of success. Short filmmakers who wish to be successful generally do not have the time and space to play around with structure in the way that Quentin Tarantino does. Playing with time lines and juggling storytelling sequence can cause confusion in a short film because of the limited timeframe available. However, it's often a feature of experimental films.

THE 'JOKE' STRUCTURE: SET-UP/PAYOFF

The set-up/payoff structure is the structure traditionally used by stand-up comedians to tell jokes. This type of structure is most commonly found in 'short shorts' of five minutes or less. It has little or no time for character or story development and must start fast with the set-up of a simple, easily understood problem, situation or dilemma for the central, usually lone, character. The character must deal quickly with this problem and the payoff is the punchline, the climax, the way he or she has resolved or paid for the situation. Such films typically deal with a single moment in time and move at a rapid pace. The scripts for these shorts seldom run to more than a few pages and dialogue tends to be minimal.

Films using the 'joke' structure do not have to be comedies. This structure can fit many different types of genre and the payoff is as likely to be dark and disturbing, as it is to be emotionally moving, satisfying or funny. The payoff may be the conclusion of a morality tale or illustrate some proverb. They can be surprisingly difficult to get right but when done well can be very effective. Their success often hinges on a surprise; an unusual, unexpected or quirky ending that is often a twist. It is critical that the payoff is well hidden. If the audience sees it coming then the film will fall flat. Don't take so long to get to the payoff that the audience has time to figure it all out. Avoid the obvious and do something original, unexpected or shocking. The payoff has to be worth the wait.

Jeff Stark's 1999 Silver Bear winner *Desserts*, which is available on YouTube, is a good example of this technique. In this two-and-a-half-minute film a man, Ewan McGregor, walks along a beach and finds a very tempting looking chocolate éclair sitting like a present on the beach. He picks it up, examines it, cautiously tastes it, then takes a bite and is immediately hooked in the mouth and dragged into the sea by unseen sea creatures 'fishing' for humans!

The 2010 Virgin Media Shorts winner, *Sign Language*, and the audience award winner, *Bus Baby*, are another two classic examples. At the time of writing they are available to watch on the Virgin Media Shorts website. Pixar's three-minute Oscar winner *For The Birds* is an animated example, while one of the best recent examples is the six-minute 2009 French film, *Toute Ma Vie* or *The Story Of My Life*. Alessandra walks across the Pont Alexandre III in Paris and is hailed by a man she doesn't recognise who seems to know everything about her. This intriguing story is capped by a shock ending and is well worth the watch.

These shorts, which resemble sketches, are growing in popularity as 'Cell Cinema' takes hold of the mobile-phone market. The 'Internet on the go' is fertile ground for this type of short filmmaking.

TRADITIONAL THREE-ACT STRUCTURE

Most short films and all the longer ones – 10 to 40 minutes – follow the traditional three-act linear structure with a beginning, middle and end sometimes referred to as a 'set-up-confrontation-resolution' structure. It's basic storytelling technique applied to the short-film format. Of course, this does not mean that you should try to squeeze a feature into a short, even if they do bear a resemblance to sequences in longer films. However, as with *District 9,* a cleverly written short film with a great idea at its heart can inspire a feature film. Writers should always keep this in mind.

These 'traditional' short films offer much greater dramatic scope to the writer, director and actors to ply their trade. The broader canvas allows for greater character, story and plot development. Generally, on the festival circuit, it's films like these that are the most successful and win the majority of the awards. Some analysts call them 'academy shorts' because of their propensity to win Oscars. Audiences and festival juries like a good story well told.

The beginning in these longer shorts is often compressed to little more than a few minutes to quickly hook the audience and propel them into the heart of the story. The division of time between the three acts and the way they are structured warrant a great deal of care from the writer and director. It's important to note that the story should move fluidly between these acts. They are not visibly separate or distinct. Every beat of the story must be carefully plotted, paying particular attention to pace.

I recommend that writers should peruse the lists of winners and nominees in the live-action categories of major festivals and awards such as the Oscars, BAFTAs, Berlin, Venice, Sundance, Cannes and specialist short-film festivals such as Clermont Ferrand and Tampere to find quality examples of these types of shorts. Many are available on compilation DVDs or the Internet. Some recent classic examples include Andrea Arnold's 26-minute *Wasp* and Martin McDonagh's 27-minute *Six Shooter*, both of which won Oscars and propelled their respective writer-directors into successful feature-film careers. This book also includes the original screenplays for two other recent Oscar-nominated short films, Juanita Wilson's *The Door* and Michael Creagh's *The Crush*.

EXPERIMENTAL FILMS

Every year festivals receive a small but significant number of submissions that are labelled 'experimental'. This usually signals that the film has little or no story and indicates that it breaks filmmaking rules and conventions in some way. It sometimes raises the suspicion that the director doesn't really know what it is.

Experimental films typically emanate from art schools, film schools and the studios of professional artists and animators. They usually feature a lot of abstract, artistic, surreal and often beautiful imagery, are frequently animated and are often based on a single clever idea or concept that repeats in a variety of guises throughout the film. They often demonstrate a lot of creativity, diversity and imagination with long moody 'hold' shots, repetitive editing, a non-linear style and minimal action. There may also be a strong philosophical, lyrical or poetic dimension running through them.

One of the most famous, or perhaps infamous, experimental films was Luis Buñuel and Salvador Dali's 16-minute *Un Chien Andalou* in 1929. Famous for its horrific eyeball-slitting scene, its bizarre and incomprehensible images provoked widely divergent, even violent, responses from audiences and critics alike.

Unfortunately, the harsh reality is that experimental films often struggle to find an audience. Art for art's sake can be too abstract and self-indulgent to connect with audiences unless they are devotees of that particular art. To hold an audience's interest, experimental films need to produce a continuous flow of clever, innovative, startling and thought-provoking ideas and images throughout the film. In reality, few do, and most tend to drag on long after their initial intriguing idea has worn thin.

Generally, arty experimental films, no matter how good, do not engage audiences. Their true home is in art galleries as video-art exhibits or in festivals with experimental-film categories where they can be properly appreciated by their peers. Of course, there is art in cinema but, for most audiences, it is the art of storytelling. There is often little to employ the skills of the dramatic screenwriter in this kind of film and they are often based more on cleverly drawn storyboards and shot lists than scripts.

In their defence, however, it must be said that experimental films are very much the research and development department of the film industry. Their pioneering value cannot be underestimated and many of the filmmaking techniques and special effects used in film today, especially in music videos and commercials, originated from, and were developed in, the world of experimental short film. However, their general lack of narrative undermines their impact both in terms of winning industry attention and major awards. What does an experimental film say as a calling card to the film industry? Often, that the filmmaker doesn't understand the harsh commercial realities of film or the audience's deep desire for story. Ultimately, in film, story is king.

LENGTH

How long should my short screenplay be? What's the ideal length for a successful short? Indeed, how long is a piece of string? It very much depends on the story you want to tell and what you want to do with it. It's often argued that there's an appropriate length to every story. It should be long enough to tell its story effectively but not so long that it drags or so short that it leaves out important story elements, but what that length should be is very much open to debate. Could you tell the story of *Dr Zhivago* in 10 minutes or stretch the story of *Desserts* to 20?

It's essential that the writer really knows his craft and structures his story in such a way that it can be told succinctly while retaining all that makes it emotionally interesting and fascinating. The writer needs to be able to judge what's essential and what can be cut. Remember: whatever the length of your short screenplay, every minute – no, every second – must be good. Your film must be tightly scripted and edited. It must be the absolute best you can produce. Economical storytelling is the key. Don't waste a second on 'fat'. Boring the audience is the cardinal sin of entertainment and nowhere does this apply more than in short film.

CUT THE FAT

Typically, films over 20 minutes long struggle to be accepted into festivals because they're too long to programme. Save time and shorten length. Strip your story down to its bare essentials. Keep asking yourself, 'Do I really need this shot? Do I really need this piece of dialogue?' If not, cut it. Cut all 'fat' from the script before you film and then do the same again during filming and editing. Don't bore your audience by dragging out scenes, adding unnecessary shots or long introductions and transitions. Excess doesn't work in shorts. The cutting has to start in the screenplay.

Follow the dictum 'enter late and leave early' when scripting scenes. Decide what each scene is about then enter the scene as late as possible, make your point, then leave as early as you can. Follow that dictum and you will create a tight script moving at a fast pace. Every scene is a building block in the story you're telling and each scene has a purpose – a point that it needs to make. Your writing needs to focus on that point then, when it has been made, move on to the next scene. Don't hang around; get out quickly. Something of relevance must happen in each scene; if not, it's redundant. Cut, trim, tighten all the time as you write and rewrite.

BUDGETS, FUNDING AND FESTIVALS

Budgets, funding agencies and festival-submission criteria all restrict screenplay length. You need to take this into account while writing. All festival and screenplay competitions set maximum – and sometimes minimum – lengths for entries. Many set generous upper limits of 40 minutes, but some, like Cannes or the British Short Screenplay Competition, set maximum 15-minute limits. Competitions for mobile-phone 'short shorts' and some ultra-short-film festivals have upper submission limits as low as two or three minutes. Hence, if you intend to write for one of these, it's essential you stay within the proscribed limit.

Funding organisations usually set page or time limits on the length of screenplays that they will accept. You will need to tailor the length of your screenplay to take this into account. The longer the screenplay, the greater it will cost to shoot it. Camera set-ups cost money. Budgets constrain length. That's the harsh reality of filmmaking.

It can be very difficult to persuade a festival programmer to accept a film over 20 minutes in length. To succeed, it really has to stand out from the crowd. Competition programmers have limited screen time available and prefer to screen a larger number of shorter films. You have a better chance of being selected if the film is less than 15 minutes long.

SHORT SHORTS OR DRAMA

Ultimately, your decision on length comes down to whether you wish to break into commercials, the mobile-phone market, sketch comedy, music promos and similar, or whether your goal is to write drama for television and film. If it's the former then 'short shorts' of less than five or six minutes are the area for you. On the other hand, if you want to break into long-form drama then 'longer' shorts of anything from 10 to 30 minutes will be more appropriate to your needs. This length suits dramatic storytelling and is the length that appeals most to ambitious rising directors, actors and writers trying to make their name. It's the length that wins awards and is most appropriate to the needs of the industry. It makes the most effective calling card.

Finally, to sum up, the following table shows the average length of live-action short-film award winners at some of the most influential film festivals and award ceremonies over the 20 years to 2009.

OSCARS	1990 to 2009	25.5 minutes
BAFTA (Winners)	1990 to 2009	16.5 minutes
BAFTA (Nominees)	1990 to 2009	15.0 minutes
VENICE (Silver Lion)	1990 to 2009	18.1 minutes
CANNES (Palme D'Or)	1989 to 2009	10.8 minutes

Note, these are averages; some winners were shorter while others were much longer. For example, two Oscar winners in 1995 and 2003 were 39 minutes long while one of the shortest Oscar winners was the eight-minute French film, *Omnibus*, in 1970. BAFTA entrants have been gradually getting shorter in recent years while Cannes limits entries to 15 minutes or less. In general, American shorts are longer than European. Study the successful if you want a guide to structure and length but remember, ultimately, it's the excellence of the screenplay and story that wins the award and recognition. We will now look at story.

5. STORY IS KING

The key to a good short screenplay is finding and telling an emotionally gripping and fascinating story. This must be your starting point. The lack of a well-developed story lies at the heart of most short films that fail. Find a story worth telling, develop it to the 'n'th degree, then write the best screenplay you can before you ever consider shooting it. Don't rush into production prematurely. Festival programmers often see films with great ideas whose potential has been squandered by clumsy storytelling and a bad script. Don't forget: at the end of the day, screenwriters are storytellers and story is king.

THE ATTRACTION OF STORY

Storytelling is as old as mankind itself. Ever since man learned to talk and communicate he's told stories by every means possible whether verbally around campfires or through cave drawings, poetry and song, painting and art, in print and now on screen. Human beings are fascinated by story. It lies at the heart of all human history.

Stories teach us about life, about people, about the world around us, and the things that can happen and have happened. Stories teach us how to dream and imagine the future. They challenge us to think about the perils of living in a dangerous and unpredictable universe. They teach us how to live and deal with seemingly insurmountable problems.

They speak to us about life and death, laughter and tears. They teach us about good and evil, morality and immorality, about justice and injustice, love, joy and the pursuit of happiness. They teach us how to slay the dragon and face the impossible with courage and fortitude. The best stories challenge us to think – what is it to be human?

Our job as short-screenplay writers is to find stories appropriate in scale and scope to the short-film medium that do any of the above. A good story should make us feel emotion. It should make us think and send us out of the cinema wondering about the world around us.

WHAT MAKES A STORY?

A number of elements go together to make a story. At its simplest a story can be defined as follows: someone wants something very badly and is having great difficulty achieving it. They have a problem and a goal. Someone or something is preventing them from getting it. He or she must struggle against great odds and an ever-increasing series of obstacles to overcome this opposition and reach his or her goal. This someone is known as the protagonist or hero and should be an interesting and emotionally engaging character, someone we can empathise with.

The greatest obstacle facing them will be the antagonist who can be either a person – the villain, bad guy, love rival – or a thing – a shark, alien, volcano, terminator, big business. The drama in the story comes primarily from the conflict between the protagonist and antagonist, from the stakes involved, and also from any secondary conflicts involving those around them. The protagonist is strongly motivated, unwilling to compromise and will do almost anything to achieve his goal, or die heroically trying. The plot tells us how the character struggles to achieve their goal. It's the vehicle for telling the story in an entertaining way.

The story must be emotionally compelling and have an emotional impact on the audience. Generally, we emotionally engage with and follow the protagonist throughout the story. He or she has a goal to achieve and is intensely motivated to pursue it at any cost. Their motives can be simple or complex but must be unrelenting. Their opponent too will have a goal, one that conflicts with that of the protagonist. The villain needs to be a well-drawn character as strong heroes need worthy opponents.

Conflict and struggle lie at the heart of all great drama. Where possible, there should be escalating struggle, increasing complications, rising tension and a rollercoaster of emotions. The stakes need to be high with great rewards for success and a high price for failure. When it's life or death, losing is not an option. Stories can have happy endings, unhappy endings or open and unresolved endings – welcome to the world of serials, sequels and, indeed, real life.

In a short there is little room for the degree of character development that would normally occur within a feature film or novel. Inevitably, the main character's struggle and development must be much simpler. Anything the character does needs to make sense within the limited story time available. Because of this difficulty most shorts focus on a single character dealing with one big problem over a relatively brief period of time. We learn about the character through his actions and the decisions he makes. Resolving powerful dilemmas produces great drama in stories and can be particularly effective in short films. Another approach is to create a serious predicament for the character then watch as she tries to overcome it and continue her quest to achieve her goal.

In sum, stories concern highly motivated characters in conflict struggling to achieve mutually incompatible goals against impossible odds and difficulty for the highest of stakes. The story will end in a climax that will change their lives for ever.

STORY TYPES

Over the years literary analysts have tried to classify stories into a number of fixed story types using a variety of criteria such as conflict, plot, theme and character type. They believe that, ultimately, all stories can be reduced to one of these simple categories. However, while there may be a finite number of story types it is clear that there are an infinite number of ways to tell them and so writers will always be able to find interesting ways to make them play out. The short-screenplay writer can use these story types as a source of inspiration when searching for and developing a suitable story.

One of the most well-known classifications is the seven-plot model. It is particularly useful because of its emphasis on conflict. Note that the 'man' in this model is not gender specific and refers to mankind in general. The seven types are as follows:

- Man versus Man
- Man versus Nature
- Man versus the Environment
- Man versus Machine or Technology
- Man versus the Supernatural
- Man versus Self
- Man versus God or Religion

Another famous classification is George Polti's *Thirty-Six Dramatic Situations*, which offers a significantly more complex analysis of story type but again it provides plenty of useful ideas for short screenplay plots. His full analysis can be found in PDF form on the Internet and downloaded for free.

Yet another is Ronald Tobias's book *20 Master Plots*, which lists 20 basic story types including quest, adventure, pursuit, rescue, escape, revenge, temptation, transformation, love, sacrifice, discovery and many more. If we take revenge as an example, it can be the basis for epics such as *Gladiator* or it can just as easily inspire a short film about a six-year-old boy taking a humorous and imaginative revenge on a classmate for breaking his favourite toy or even an angry wife punishing a philandering husband. It's all a matter of scale and applying the story type creatively to a subject that can be told in, say, 10 minutes, while working within the limits of the filmmaker's resources.

Then there are the myths and legends, fairytales, folk tales and fables, and even the Bible, all of which contain story ideas that can be adapted to the writer's needs. Hollywood itself has its own story categorisation system known as genre, which breaks film stories down into types such as crime, thriller, romance, drama, action, adventure, comedy, mystery, sci-fi, western and so on, with subgenres in each category.

A MOMENT IN TIME

The biggest problem faced by writers telling a story in short-screenplay format is timescale. Many short screenplays tell a story based on a single moment in time – everything takes place in a single day. This can significantly limit the types of stories that can be told. There may be no room for the pursuit of a significant long-term goal so many short films focus entirely on one character trying to resolve a short-term problem or difficulty – a negative goal – removing a problem rather than achieving something.

They're faced with a predicament, a crisis, a sudden problem or dilemma and their only goal is to find a way out of it and return to normality. This can produce perfectly effective stories but it lacks the sense of purpose of a character pursuing a positive goal and struggling to get somewhere. The longer the short film and screenplay, the more room there is to tell a bigger story spread over a longer timeframe.

The typical short screenplay will concentrate on only one or two key characters and have a leaner, more condensed narrative. It will be tighter and focus on a single main storyline. Typically, there will be an emphasis on visual presentation with little dialogue. All attention will focus on the individual with the most immediate or tangible problem, which he or she will struggle to resolve over the course of the screenplay.

NO BORING BITS, PLEASE!

Hitchcock once said that drama is life with the boring bits cut out. Unfortunately, many short filmmakers do the exact opposite and tell bland stories about the dull, mundane, everyday bits of life with dialogue that is every bit as bad. People go to the cinema to escape from the boredom of everyday life. They go to live for a time in a different world or body and experience things that normally they could only dream of. They go to be emotionally challenged, excited, entertained and thrilled.

Short filmmakers and writers need to understand this and write stories that cater to this need. Short doesn't have to mean dull. Be ambitious with what you've got, push the boundaries and tell a great story. Drama is all around us. Find it and adapt it to your needs and resources. The cardinal sin of filmmaking and storytelling is to create boredom. You must never bore the audience. Be dramatic, take it to the extreme and tell a story that creates a powerful emotional experience for the audience, one that they will find deeply satisfying.

STORY ESSENTIALS

In scripting your story don't forget to follow the essential rules of storytelling and carefully consider the following points:

- You MUST have a strong beginning. Begin fast, hook the viewer and set your story up quickly.

- You MUST create emotional involvement and engage with the audience.

- Create memorable characters that actors will kill to play. Be original and avoid clichés, stereotypes and one-dimensional characters. Give us something we haven't seen before.

- Establish your character and his or her 'world' early. Are they empathetic? Will we care for them emotionally?

- What is the central problem or dilemma facing the character? What is his or her goal? What do they want?

- What obstacles do they face? How will they overcome them, if at all?

- What are the stakes? Are they life and death? Is there real dramatic tension or suspense? Is there enough conflict? Will it leave the audience clinging to the edge of their seats?

- Who or what is the antagonist? Draw him, her or it well. Heroes need strong enemies and worthy opponents.

- Write sparkling, clever dialogue with memorable quotes, witty exchanges and clever subtext. Leave out the dull, aimless chatter of everyday life and avoid excessive talking heads.

- If your script is dialogue heavy, reconsider. Do you really need all of it? If you plan to submit to foreign festivals you will need subtitles but excessive dialogue does not work well with subtitles. It distracts from the visuals.

- Who are your target audience? What do you want them to remember about your short? What do you want them to say about your film as they walk out of the cinema?

- Be visual. Conjure up powerful, evocative images. Remember the 'WOW' factor.

- Don't forget pace. Never let your short drag, especially in the middle. Keep up the momentum, especially if it is long.

- Be clever with comedy and avoid schoolboy humour or anything that might be considered extremely offensive or blasphemous, especially in other cultures. Comedy doesn't travel well.

- Don't repel, revolt or disgust your audience with extremely repulsive, vulgar or crude scenes of things such as vomiting, violence and mutilation, hardcore sexual images and bodily functions. Is the sex and violence gratuitous? Think of your audience. Festival audiences are generally very liberal, open-minded and tolerant but nevertheless there is a limit. Festivals do get some very extreme material. We're talking really extreme, over-the-top material, not just run-of-the-mill nudity, sex, violence or bad language. There's shock and there's SHOCK!

- Don't forget your budget, if any. Think of the practicalities. Cost escalates with the number of characters and locations, night shoots, stunts and special effects, elaborate costumes and settings, guns and weapons or any kind of pyrotechnic or CGI.

- Why are you writing this screenplay? Is there a moral to the story? Are you trying to entertain or are you trying to communicate a serious message about your chosen topic? How will you do that subtly without preaching? The most powerful shorts are those that make you think.

- Finish well and end on a high. Will the ending make you cry, cheer, laugh or smile for all the right reasons? The climax needs to be powerful, emotionally satisfying and worth the wait. Audiences like surprise endings but don't twist just for the sake of it. Predictable and clichéd twists can backfire. On the other hand, brilliantly executed, original and totally unexpected twists delight audiences and are always remembered (e.g. *The Sixth Sense*, *The Crying Game* and *The Usual Suspects*).

To conclude, if you want to write a great screenplay and make a standout short film find a story worth telling, one appropriate to the short-film format, and develop it to the full. Be ambitious, be dramatic and never be boring. Don't forget you're trying to create an unforgettable calling card that will help to establish you in the eyes of the industry as a professional screenwriter and filmmaker. The primary audience for short film is the industry itself. Never forget it's all about story, story, story! Story is king!

6. FINDING A STORY

How do you find a story worth telling? Where do you get your inspiration? How do you generate ideas? Alan Ball said that his inspiration for *American Beauty* came from watching news coverage of the Amy Fisher-Joey Buttafuoco trial and a chance encounter with a plastic bag blowing in the wind outside the World Trade Centre. François Truffaut said, '20 per cent of my material is autobiographical, 20 per cent comes from newspapers, 20 per cent from people I know and 20 per cent is pure fiction. The rest? Fiction does not play a major part. I prefer to work with real life.'

OPEN YOUR MIND

In reality, ideas and inspiration are all around us but you may not notice unless you make a conscious effort to look for them. You need to become a magnet for ideas, always receptive, always searching. Fine tune your story antenna and open your mind. Ideas can come from your memories, life experience, job or daily wanderings, from overheard bits of conversation and things you see around you, from newspapers or magazines, television or the Internet, from children and relatives, daydreams and gossip, short stories, paintings, photos, songs, books in libraries or the wildest thought that pops into your brain from some unidentifiable place in the ether. They can come from anywhere. You must be ready to recognise them and their potential when they appear.

Learn to look in the right places. If you're interested in crime writing look through newspapers for crime stories, read court reports, go and sit in the public gallery when a court is in session, listen and think. Look in local papers for the 'small' crime dramas or trawl newspaper archives in libraries. An incident from 100 years ago may contain the seeds of a story, not in its historical setting, but in the conflict, motives and emotions of the key participants.

If you like stories about the sea go and talk to fishermen, coast-guards, lifeboat men, study life in a fishing port, research what they do, the lives they live and the emergencies they've had to deal with. Talk to their relatives who stay ashore and worry; their worries may contain the seeds of a story. Look for the unusual, the drama in their lives. Do the same with whatever subject catches your interest.

Look for ideas that capture your imagination because they unlock a powerful emotion. Think about how the idea makes you feel. Emotions are powerful creative triggers and engines in storytelling. Look for the emotional truth, the 'heart', in an idea and think of the story you could write from it. Ask yourself: could I touch the audience with this?

Shorts can be about anything so there's no limit to the imagination but think about the practical limits on time, the number of characters and locations, the need to be visual, the budget, the need for conflict, struggle, choices. Watch a lot of shorts to see what's already been done to death, the clichés and stereotypes, and then try to do something different. Screen out overdone and worn out ideas.

Ask questions about everything. What would happen if this happened? What would I do if that happened? What if someone recreated dinosaurs from their DNA? What would you do for one million dollars? What would happen if I was dead and didn't know it? Ask 'what if' questions about everything.

ASSESS THE DRAMATIC POTENTIAL

Anything can spark an idea. You need to collect them on paper and assess their dramatic potential. Think of the ingredients of story from the last chapter and ask, do any of these ideas fit? Do they suggest conflict, struggle or an interesting problem? Is there a hook or good ending? Do they stir an emotion or make you think about life, people, anything?

Train yourself to think visually and assess every idea's visual potential. You're writing for a medium where the camera tells the story. Think about its emotional power. We go to the cinema looking for an emotional experience. Ultimately, it's the emotional connection with the story and its characters that will decide whether we feel the experience has been worthwhile. Evaluate each idea and ask, is there a story?

Ideas are just the raw material; they all need work to turn them into stories. Decide which of them has the potential to make a good story and which fits the requirements of a short screenplay. Filter them. Exclude the dull and mundane, the clichés, the unexciting and those with no visual possibilities. Some are so big only a feature film or novel could do them justice while others won't contain enough potential for growth. Some will only contain enough for a brief 'joke'-structure-type short but some will contain the story elements you need.

PERSONAL INTERESTS

You will find that your own passions and interests will shape your storytelling and focus your attention onto some ideas more than others. It'll help you to filter ideas and will influence the shape and direction of the stories you subsequently tell. That's fine so long as your story is dramatic and emotionally strong enough for the screen. Sometimes the same idea can be taken in many different directions, happy or sad. Many writers have particular preferences; some like crime or romance while others like horror and so on.

However, if your passion is stamp collecting or trainspotting, don't expect the audience to share your fascination unless you're a psychotic collector who's stealing priceless stamps from all over the world for your own jealously guarded private collection, or you're a private detective or insurance investigator pursuing such a person. If you're a trainspotter you'd better stumble upon the great train robbery or witness a murder and be pursued through the train networks you love by the murderers trying to silence you.

In other words, whatever the setting, whatever your interest, you must find the drama in it and turn it into something emotionally exciting that engages and entertains an audience. Shorts have to work the same way. Pick a suitable idea, one that fits the timescale and constraints of a short, then make it as intense and dramatic as you can within the confines of that space. Blend your passions and interests with a real dramatic story.

IDEAS FOLDER

Keep an ideas folder or shoebox and add all those little scribbled notes, ideas for a title or a line of dialogue, newspaper cuttings or whatever, to it. Don't let good ideas slip through your fingers because you failed to write them down. Keep little notebooks or memo pads handy in the glove compartment of your car, beside your bed, in an office drawer, or in a jacket pocket or handbag. When an idea hits, write it down immediately then add it to your folder. If you don't, it will be lost.

The mind only retains things temporarily in the short-term memory. The ongoing mental activity of everyday life constantly drives things out of the short-term memory. It takes effort to transfer something into the long-term memory. If you're too busy to do that, your unwritten idea will quickly be pushed out and forgotten. The very act of writing something down helps to bed things down in the mind.

If it's an idea that really excited you, scribble extra notes, expand on it and add those to your folder as well. It's good practice to date those notes and add some sort of identifying title so you can later collate separate notes you've made about that idea. Every now and then look through the folder and sift through your ideas, pulling out the ones that really excite you. Now you've material for a short screenplay or maybe even a feature. Keep unused notes. You never know when they might trigger something useful, even years from now. Ideas are the lifeblood of writers.

Periodically revisit your ideas folder, think about the ideas in it and expand the notes you've already accumulated. The ideas that grow the most have 'legs' and show the greatest story potential. Try mixing different ideas together and ask – can I make a story from that? I find visiting my ideas folders particularly productive when I'm mentally blocked on another project. The very act seems to generate new material in the ideas folder while strangely it also unblocks my mind when I return to the project I was originally working on. The ideas folder is your witch's cauldron brewing up ideas. It's a melting pot for stories.

WRITE WHAT YOU KNOW

I believe this is one of the most misleading pieces of advice given to writers and filmmakers today. It has become a cliché and is responsible for producing many of the dull stories that festival programmers see every year during short-film viewings and selection. It denies and subverts the power of the writer's imagination, creativity, ingenuity and research. It undervalues the talent of professional writers. It sends beginning writers and filmmakers scurrying down a dark alleyway of uninspired filmmaking as they misinterpret this phrase to mean that they should make films based on their 'normal' lives, everyday lifestyle and locale.

If you're an average member of the public your life is generally pretty ordinary, unexciting and lacking in drama. If you live a peaceful stable life where nothing dramatic ever happens or are a film student just starting out on life what do you write about? You need a lot of life experience and, indeed, chaos in your life to have a story worth telling. When life runs smoothly there is no drama. There's nothing to inspire the great stories that the rest of us want to watch. People go to the cinema to escape from the dreariness and boredom of everyday life, not to see it regurgitated on screen.

However, that said, there is another side to this phrase that is indeed appropriate and usually misunderstood. One thing you do know, we all know, is what it is to be human. Every one of us knows what it is to laugh, cry, feel pain, hunger, anger, grief, joy, love and so on; in short, what it is to feel and experience human emotions. We all know the primal needs of hunger and thirst, warmth and shelter, love and desire, sex and procreation, the survival instinct and protection of loved ones, fear of death and so on. These are the things you do know that you need to write about. Focus your attention on your knowledge of human emotion.

Jaws capitalised on this. The fear of sharks, being eaten by monsters from the deep, is primal. It is universally understood. There's no one on Earth who didn't immediately get this. Spielberg successfully tapped into this primal emotion and created what is now seen as the first of the film industry's summer blockbusters.

In writing what you know think about your most intimate and personal emotions and experiences. What did they feel like? Now transfer that to the characters and imaginary situations in your story. Create emotional situations that will touch an audience using all that you've learned and know of human emotions. That's where the connection with the audience lies. Your first kiss or love, the tragic loss of a loved one, a painful divorce, grief, the loss of a parent or child, the elation or joy of winning some great success, getting married, the birth of a child and so on. Think about your own deeply emotional experiences and what they meant for you then transfer that emotion to your stories. Now you're writing about what you know. Mix it with creativity, imagination and the rest of your storytelling talent to create something special.

Alan Ball, writer of *American Beauty*, commented, 'Write what you care about, write what moves you, what intrigues you and you find compelling, write what angers you and makes you sad.'

IMAGINATION, CREATIVITY, RESEARCH

An essential part of any writing process is the writer's ability to use his or her imagination and creativity to craft a fascinating story from the various ideas and storytelling ingredients at his or her disposal. If you want to write about a particular subject but lack the knowledge to do it then research it. Use the vast information resources available today to find out what you need to know to add depth, realism, quality and believability to your story. It might be a location, an occupation or some real event that's the backdrop to your story, a costume, prop or technique, whatever. If necessary, research it. Find what you need. Research adds authenticity to any story.

All great writers use their imagination, creativity and emotional intelligence to blend ideas taken from reality with imaginary elements to create new, exciting and entertaining stories. They don't just write what they know. Stephen King doesn't live with demons, devils and supernatural creatures. Thomas Harris wasn't a liver-eating serial killer. David Franzoni wasn't a Roman gladiator, and Steven Spielberg didn't meet an extra-terrestrial in his back garden or fight the shark from hell. Dan O'Bannon didn't live on a space freighter and fight alien monsters with acid for blood. They all made use of their knowledge of human emotion and some real-life events which they'd researched then added their imagination and creativity to create successful stories. These weren't the worlds they knew or lived in; they were the worlds they created by blending fact, fiction, research, imagination, creativity and their knowledge of human emotion. When writing your short screenplay you need to do the same, albeit on a smaller canvas.

DRAMA

People go to the cinema to escape from boredom. They go to be excited, entertained, thrilled and even to fantasise that they're one of the characters up there on screen living out a life infinitely more exciting than their own. They go to see drama. Where do we find it? Drama springs from unusual events and extraordinary situations, from crisis, conflict and dilemma, from life being turned upside down. When life runs smoothly there is no drama. Drama occurs when the abnormal happens. It subverts normality, so take the normal and inject the abnormal. Create an intolerable situation for the protagonist. Avoid the ordinary and give us the extraordinary.

You, as a writer, must do the exact same thing when creating a story and writing your short screenplay. Take your ideas and normal world then add a catalyst, an abnormal event that has unexpected or unpredictable consequences. It changes the principal character's life and gives him or her a serious problem to deal with. Now add your imagination, creativity and whatever research you need to create conflict, difficulties and dilemmas for the characters. Give them goals, powerful motives and dangerous opponents. Walk them through hell and see what they do. Be original. Be ambitious. Take it to the extreme and take your characters and the audience on an emotional rollercoaster ride. Now we have a story.

All drama involves conflict, struggle and high stakes. Give us drama, and please – no boring bits.

7. BRAINSTORMING – GENERATING STORIES

In this chapter I will look at some worked examples of finding an idea and brainstorming a story. I could've selected ideas from any of the other sources mentioned in the previous chapters but for this exercise I've deliberately chosen some fairly innocuous and unexciting items from local newspapers just to see what can be done. Normally I'd be doing the reverse, i.e. seeking the most interesting and dramatic ideas, but for the sake of this exercise I thought it would be more interesting to make it difficult and see whether I could still create drama from even quite unpromising ideas. Anything goes when you're looking for an idea to kick-start a story.

In this case, the four things I've selected were an advertisement for a shoe shop, a photo of a local postmistress retiring surrounded by well-wishers, a news item about a gas explosion collapsing a shop and injuring three people, and a photo of an upturned car lying in a ditch at the bottom of a small embankment on a country road. What on earth could I do with these? They're not exactly stand-out things. Two contain some drama – an explosion and a crash – but the other two? It'll be an interesting challenge.

I took a sheet of paper for each and began brainstorming. When you brainstorm, take the lid off your imagination and let the ideas genie or demon out of the bottle. Let it all burst forth. Think sideways, twisted, outside the box. Don't stop to criticise any idea while brainstorming, there's plenty of time for that later. Right now you just want every potential idea out on the table no matter how wild or daft it sounds. Let them flow, don't be conservative, don't be afraid. There might be a hidden gem in there. Your own interests, passions or preferences might influence this process but try to keep an open mind. I love film noir, crime drama and political and psychological thrillers so I'll not be surprised if some of my story ideas veer in those directions.

Once you've compiled a list of possible dramatic stories for each topic, reassess and decide which shows the most dramatic potential. Which could be filmed as a short within the limits of your budget and resources? Test your list on friends to see which suggestions generate the most response. Okay, let's start with our shoe shop.

THE SHOE SHOP STORY

I selected the shoe-shop advert deliberately to represent those who take 'write what you know' literally. It would represent a writer who works part time in a shoe shop and is trying to write a story based on their working life. I've never worked in a shoe shop myself, by the way. So let's say our writer is female and a retail assistant in a shoe shop in a large shopping centre. What kind of story could you create? You know your normal working routine and can easily paint that picture as an opening. You stock the shelves, service customers, help them find suitable shoes, facilitate their purchases, and so on. Okay, so not very exciting. Now we need to add drama. We have to do something unusual, unexpected and abnormal, then add it to the mix and stir.

PANDORA'S BOX

A customer comes in, selects shoes then asks if you have it in a different size. You go into the storeroom as you've done a thousand times before, find the box, pull it off the rack and open it, then stare in shock. No shoes. Instead it's packed full of money or drugs or a gun or a mix of all three. You stare at it. What do you do next? Now we have dilemma and drama. Who owns it? What will they do if you take it? What if you take the money home? The owner may pursue you – terror at your flat. If you give it to the police the owner might want revenge – more terror. What if you put it back but are seen by the person who put it there? Now you're a threat to be neutralised.

Suddenly the normal has become abnormal. This is the Pandora's box scenario from Greek mythology. Once opened, all the evils of the world fly out. In a situation like this you can put anything you want into that box and take the story in any direction. What if the box contains a venomous spider? Pornographic photos of a child with someone you know? Compromising documents? Some strange object with supernatural powers – *The Mask*? A DVD with something disturbing on it? A snuff video? A job offer that's very illegal? What if, while you're in the storeroom, you overhear a disturbing conversation between the shop owner and someone else? What could it be? A blackmail demand? A threat? Is he arranging the death of his wife? What if they catch you? We have an abundance of dramatic hooks. The possibilities are endless.

Let's say it's a DVD with her name on it. She returns to the shop but the strange man who asked for the shoes is gone. Puzzled, she takes the DVD home, watches it and is horrified to discover that it's all secret film of her. It includes shots of her sunbathing and undressing in her bedroom. Someone's stalking her. Was it the man in the shop? Suddenly she hears a sound at the door? Now we have a psychological thriller.

So you see we took normal, added abnormal and created a dilemma with a range of possible options, conflicts, consequences and stakes. The character must make a decision and act. We've created drama and a potentially interesting story.

LOVE, SEX AND OTHER WOES

Let's try a different tack. You're attractive, good looking, and the male or, indeed, female owner sexually harasses and assaults you in the storeroom. You reject his or her advances and threaten them with the police. They stop but are clearly annoyed and worried. Suddenly, next day, they call you in and tell you they're sacking you for stealing. They're lying, of course, and covering their back so that if you go to the police or their partner they can claim you're just making it up to get revenge for being sacked. But you're innocent, aggrieved and want to fight back. Now we have the makings of a story – a strong goal, i.e. your need to prove your innocence, a clear conflict, high stakes, an antagonist and drama. How do you prove your innocence? There's plenty of scope for a dramatic story.

Let's try a love story. You serve an attractive young man who flirts with you. You've noticed him about the shop before and fancy him. You help him select a pair of distinctive shoes but the entire conversation is actually a thinly disguised romantic chat up. This would be great as an exercise in subtext. Use a clever play on words, perhaps disguised as a sales pitch, accompanied by suitable looks and body language, to indicate that what is really going on is a romantic courtship dance. The end result of the conversation is a 'sale', which is really an agreement to go out with him on a date that night. He leaves all smiles in his new shoes.

You're on top of the world and go on an early dinner break. As you leave the shopping centre you hear sirens. You turn a corner to see a crowd gathered, an ambulance and police. There's been a fatal road accident. Someone's been run over. A sheet covers the body. You move closer to look, only to see a pair of legs sticking out from under the sheet wearing the exact same shoes you've just sold. It's a shock ending and twist. Spot my dark and twisted film noir mind? I'm intrigued, though, by the thought of creating a romantic chat up that is all subtext. Remember the chess scene from *The Thomas Crown Affair*. It would be interesting if it could be made to work.

Perhaps you're having an affair with the owner of the shop. It's a love triangle and his wife finds out. He ropes you into a conspiracy to get rid of her; maybe she's wealthy and he profits? What if the triangle is between you and another girl who also works in the shop, with the storeroom the scene of your sexual encounters? Your love rival catches the two of you together and in a rage she does what? More drama.

I bet you never realised so much went on in a shoe shop! This was all inspired by a simple newspaper advert. Look at the variety and range of potential stories and drama brainstorming has produced. I'm sure a few of them are more than viable as ideas for a short screenplay; one or two might even trigger a feature, e.g. the stalker DVD one. Let's try our next scenario.

THE POSTMISTRESS

I decided to combine the retiring postmistress picture with the little news story about a gas explosion collapsing a shop and injuring three people. What can I do with this?

It's retirement day and the postmistress is busy at work in her little post office, serving customers and receiving presents and farewell cards from friends. It's clear she's very popular and much loved. Along with her is John who's known and worked with her 30 years. They're the best of friends. It's obvious he's also very sorry to see her go. We show normality, their routine and friendship, but now we throw the joker into the mix, something abnormal to create drama, the gas.

John goes into the little kitchen at the back to make them their usual dinnertime snack. He smells gas. There's a leak. He gets a torch to look. Just then the postmistress walks into the kitchen and opens the fridge. She turns the light switch as she does so. John yells a warning but it's too late – BANG! All we need to show onscreen is a flash of white accompanied by a realistic-sounding blast then blackness and the sound of masonry and debris falling followed by silence.

As we fade up from darkness to a dusty half-light, we hear groaning. The postmistress is trapped in a pocket under the wreckage. She has light from the partially crushed fridge that lies half open. You need to write in some light – don't forget someone has to be able to film it.

Trapped but not badly hurt she calls out to John then sees his arm and a hand sticking out from other wreckage. She calls to him and after a moment he answers. He's okay, he says, hurt, trapped but alive. Talk to me. She edges closer until she can hold his hand. They begin to talk. He tells her how much he'll miss her when she's gone then he begins to tell her that he loves her and has always loved her. Under the wreckage, for the first time he finally reveals his true feelings for her. He's been too shy to say it all these years. She's overcome with emotion and promises him it'll all be different when they get out of this wreckage. As he talks we hear the noise of rescuers clearing the rubble.

Suddenly they clear a space around her and free her but she won't let go of John's hand. The rescuers try to persuade her to let go. 'I'm sorry love, he's gone'... 'He can't be, I was just talking to him'... 'I'm sorry love, that's not possible, the concrete beam, it... he must've died instantly. He didn't suffer.' John's been dead all along. She's been talking to his ghost. She's helped away stunned and in tears. Now we have a love story and tragedy.

The same equation, normal plus abnormal, gives drama. Two people trapped and injured, a little love story and the surprise twist; he's been dead all along. It also suggests a theme: don't leave it too late to tell someone you love them.

THE OVERTURNED CAR

This final idea came from a photo of a minor road accident. A car had left the road, rolled over and down a small embankment at the side of a remote country road. What could I do with this? It was already an abnormal situation, a car accident; what else could I add to the mix to make it more than just a routine road-traffic incident? I brainstormed a series of ideas.

They all begin with the protagonist, a man in his early thirties walking along the country road. He notices skid marks and debris at the side of the road, looks over and sees the car upturned in the ditch. There's no obvious sign of life. He slides down to it. What does he find?

The following are my story ideas:

1. He sees an arm and leg sticking out from under the car. He rolls the car over to uncover the body. The man is dead. He turns the body over and discovers that it's himself. It's the *Sixth Sense* ending and twist.

2. He gets to the car and finds there's a woman trapped in the front passenger seat. Shock, it's his wife! She's not badly hurt. The guy under the car is her lover. He appears to be dying. There's petrol leaking from the tank. She's been having an affair. He notices her suitcase in the back. She angrily tells him she's leaving him. They have a row. He lights a match, tosses it behind him and walks away. She screams after him as the car erupts in flames.

3. He finds the driver near death and in the back a large sum of money in a rucksack. He suffocates the driver, takes the bag of money and leaves. But unknown to him a second man lying injured nearby has seen it all. He recovers and pursues the man who took the money. It's the *Shallow Grave* plot.

4. He finds two injured men with guns, masks and money. They've crashed fleeing a robbery. They threaten him then offer him money to help them get away. What does he do? They're trapped. The petrol's leaking. He pretends to help but lifts the money then, like the story above, throws a match and walks away.

5. You chance upon the accident and discover the driver injured but in the boot is a dead body. The driver has crashed on his way to dispose of it. He's armed and holds you at gunpoint. He wants you to help him leave the scene but you know he'll kill you if you do. What do you do?

6. You find the driver dead but hear noises coming from the boot. You force the boot open to discover a man bound and gagged. You free him but suddenly he turns on you. He has a knife and terrorises you. It turns out he's a complete and utter psychopath and you need to trick him to escape. You do but he pursues you through the nearby forest until someone rescues you. It's the *Dead Calm*/Billy Zane scenario.

7. You caused the accident but drive away. Later you discover that the driver was alive and could've been saved but died due to lack of medical help. You're torn by guilt. Later you return by car at night to the scene but in a cruel twist of fate lose control and crash at the very same spot after swerving to avoid a figure crossing the road. You die before help can reach you but before you do you see the ghost of the man you left to die. He's laughing at you. He was the figure on the road.

These ideas above again illustrate the potential for finding stories by brainstorming. Always look for the abnormal, the drama in every situation.

REAL LIFE

Real life is often stranger than the best fiction. Think of 9/11, the Titanic, JFK's assassination, Vesuvius, Pompeii, Apollo 13, the Holocaust, Columbine, Waco and Jack the Ripper. Would anyone have believed you if you'd written these stories before they actually happened? Fact is stranger than fiction and often much more dramatic. Hollywood knows this and often takes inspiration from the real world. There's nothing stopping you as a short filmmaker from doing the same, albeit on a smaller, more localised scale. Search for the drama around you and adapt it to your needs and resources. Take the ideas you find, blend them with other ideas, then use your imagination and creativity to create something original, dramatic and emotionally involving.

8. SCREENPLAY FORMAT

What is screenplay format and why do we use it? Screenplay format is a special coded language and page layout that is universally used and understood by professionals working in the film industry. It is the written language of screenwriting. The layout and information it contains simplifies the process of turning a script from words on a page into images on a screen. It tells each department what it needs to know in order to make the film.

Why should you use it? Proper format separates the pros from the amateurs – at least that's the perception. If you want to be a professional screenwriter, start as you mean to continue, adopt professional work habits and write like a professional. Presentation does count. If you look like a professional then you're more likely to be treated as one. Proper format can't hide a badly written story but at the end of the day it's a business requirement and not hard to learn. Why penalise yourself by ignoring it?

Screenplay competitions score scripts on format. Incorrectly formatted scripts struggle to pass the first round. Many competitions won't even accept them. Agents, producers, funding bodies, indeed all industry professionals expect to see properly formatted screenplays as a norm. The belief is that if you can't format a script, you're an amateur, don't understand the business and, in all probability, don't understand how to write a story for the screen. Competition is intense so don't spoil your chances.

FORMAT DIFFERENCES

In my experience the world of short film is particularly prone to badly formatted screenplays. I've seen short scripts written in biro, on A4 note pads, typed in stage, television and radio-play formats or a mixture of all three. I've also read professionally written short screenplays and the difference is enormous. While some of the badly formatted scripts did contain good ideas, they were full of basic mistakes, difficult to read and contained a lot of things that simply couldn't be filmed.

The cause? In my opinion many of those making short films have no screenwriting ability. They don't know the basics and so don't think format matters. They fail to adequately develop their story visually on the page and the lack of coherence and clarity shows later in pre-production. A confused, badly written script can produce a confused, badly organised film shoot. Format helps to order and organise the necessary information.

Some beginning screenwriters write in the form they're most familiar with whether it's amateur dramatics, theatre, radio, television or academia. They look around for examples of screenplays and are often misled by reading scripts that are in fact shooting scripts or even just transcripts of the film's dialogue wrongly published in a theatrical format.

It's important to note that television broadcast formats differ from one type of production to another. Theatre, radio and television formats are all different because of the different production requirements of each medium. Short film belongs to the film world and so follows the same screenplay format and conventions as feature film. It's the one format that is universal.

HOLLYWOOD FORMAT

The standard screenplay format used in film today is variously known as the Standard Industry Format, the Hollywood Format or Studio

Format. It began in the earliest days of film and quickly rose to worldwide dominance with the rise of the Hollywood studio system. Its great advantage was that it produced a practical working document in a standardised form all those working in the industry could easily read and understand. The acknowledged bible of Hollywood screenplay format is *The Complete Guide to Standard Script Formats – Part 1: The Screenplay* by Hillis R Cole and Judith H Haag. It's well worth having if you plan to become a full-time professional screenwriter.

SOFTWARE PACKAGES

A range of software packages now exist that take the pain out of writing in proper format. They allow the writer to concentrate fully on the task of writing while still producing a professional-looking script. *Final Draft* and *Movie Magic Screenwriter* are the dominant, more expensive, packages but there are several others. There are also free-to-download packages available on the Internet such as *Celtx* and the BBC's *ScriptSmart Gold* which is available from its *Writersroom* website. Investing in a professional screenplay formatter is a must if you plan to become a full-time professional screenwriter.

KEY COMPONENTS AND LAYOUT

There are five key components to a screenplay that must be formatted each with its own position on the page:

SCENES

CHARACTER NAMES

ACTION or DESCRIPTION

DIALOGUE

PARENTHETICALS

A typical page layout includes a one-inch margin at top and bottom and on the right-hand side with a one-and-a-half-inch margin on the left to allow for binding. The following table summarises the usual page settings. All measurements listed below are in inches taken from the left-hand side of the page. Note, just because the character name or scene heading can go all the way to the right margin doesn't mean that it should. Both should be kept as brief and simple as possible. I have also used inches to simplify, as most guides or publications list these as Tab numbers, which can be a bit more confusing for the reader.

Component	Begins	Ends
Scene Heading	1.5	Right margin
Action/Description	1.5	Right margin
Character Name	3.5	Right margin
Parentheticals	3.0	5.0
Dialogue	2.5	6.0
Transitions	5.5	Right margin

I have included transitions above but most screenplays today dispense with them, regarding them as superfluous and implied by the presence of a new scene heading anyway.

COURIER 12 POINT

All screenplays MUST be written in Courier 12-point font. This is basic. All screenwriting software is set to use this as a default. There are two reasons, historic and practical. First, Hollywood started out using manual typewriters that used Courier 12 point as a standard typeface and this became the industry norm. However, while using it, the industry discovered that a page of properly formatted screenplay using Courier 12 point averaged one minute of screen time. Other fonts and layouts deviated from this. A page a minute therefore became a rule of thumb – a standard way to estimate a film's length and budget. However, a page a minute as an average holds up better the longer the script is. It's a less reliable guide in short screenplays where film length can deviate substantially from page length.

FADE IN/FADE OUT

All screenplays begin with FADE IN, written in the top-left-hand corner before the first scene heading, and end with FADE OUT, written on the bottom right after the last scene. THE END, centred, sometimes follows this. Fades are dissolves from, or to, black and indicate movement into or out of the story world. The reason for using these terms is partly visual – the film doesn't start and end suddenly on a cut – and partly philosophical. The world, life, history are in constant motion and exist before and after our story. The story world exists before and after we join it. We are merely dropping in, paying it a visit as it were, to follow one particular story or character. When that story is done we will leave to return to our own world. Fades indicate this fact. FADE TO BLACK, right aligned, and FADE UP, left aligned, are sometimes used mid screenplay if, for example, a character loses consciousness or goes into a dream, fantasy world or even, sometimes, into a flashback sequence.

SCENE HEADINGS

The main component of a screenplay is the scene. All scenes begin with a SCENE HEADING, also known as a Slugline, and are always written entirely in CAPITALS. Every scene heading contains three elements:

- INTERIOR or EXTERIOR always abbreviated as INT or EXT
- LOCATION
- TIME OF DAY

The scene heading must always remain attached to the description that follows it. It must not be split across pages.

INT or EXT

INTERIOR or EXTERIOR, always abbreviated, begin every scene heading. This indicates the nature of the scene to everyone involved in making the film. It tells all the creative and technical personnel the kind of scene they're going to shoot, and therefore the equipment they're likely to need, and the potential problems they might face, especially weather.

LOCATION

The location name or description is generally kept as brief as possible. It can be vague and generic or very specific and precise, for example:

INT – A HOUSE – DAY

Or

EXT – DEALEY PLAZA, DALLAS – 1220 hrs 22nd NOV 1963

The latter, of course, being just minutes before the assassination of President Kennedy. Consistency must be maintained in naming the location so that if it appears again later in the script there is no confusion. Film locations do not require the elaborate description found in a novel. The detail is left to set designers and the art department.

TIME OF DAY

The time of day is indicated by adding DAY or NIGHT after the location. This information is very important as it indicates to the film crew and filmmakers the lighting conditions and ambience that have to be replicated in the scene. The following descriptions are now also regularly used – MORNING, AFTERNOON, EVENING, DAWN, DUSK, SUNRISE, SUNSET, MIDDAY, MIDNIGHT and even NEW YEAR or CHRISTMAS as well as the four seasons. LATER, MOMENTS LATER and CONTINUOUS are also used if the time of day has already been listed in a previous scene heading. 'Continuous' is used when there is a continuous flow of action across several successive scenes and locations which are linked in time.

Precise times or even dates can be used for dramatic effect as in the Kennedy assassination example above. Time pressure is a staple ingredient of suspense in thrillers. Sometimes it's also necessary to take account of the season if it affects the degree of light available, for example, 7.30 am will look very different in summer and winter.

ACTION/DESCRIPTION

The scene heading is always followed by an action/description component. Further lines of action can also appear throughout the scene, sometimes splitting blocks of dialogue. This section is also used to introduce and describe characters, locations and other visual elements of the story as well as commenting on the time of day, weather and anything else pertinent to the scene or the actions occurring within it.

Description should always be simple, concise and to the point, with no superfluous text. It should be highly visual and deal only with what happens in the scene. It should not exceed four or five lines. Long passages should be broken up into shorter paragraphs or sentences. Producers and script readers dislike dense areas of text.

Splitting action into short single lines separated by a space can enhance pace. This is sometimes known as 'directing on the page' as it can be used to suggest shots to the director. This technique is also used for montages, which are often used as prologues or scene setters or to indicate the rapid passage of time. Such sections are introduced by using a secondary heading saying MONTAGE or SERIES OF SHOTS, followed by the desired actions listed sequentially line by line. Beware of creating redundancies. These are when the description needlessly repeats something in the header or dialogue.

CHARACTER

Characters are always introduced in the action section with a brief but memorable description. Always CAPITALISE the full name the first time it appears. This assists casting directors and actors analysing the script. The description should not be too specific as regards physical appearance – unless it contains some plot point – but should instead highlight one or two key character traits or defining characteristics that make the character stand out. Detailed physical description can cause casting problems and will probably be ignored anyway.

A character's name always appears in capitals before his or her dialogue. It's essential that each character's name remains consistent in these dialogue headings throughout the screenplay even if he or she is addressed differently by other characters in the story. Don't give different characters similar sounding names such as Terry and Jerry, John and Joan, Alan and Alex, Ned and Ed and so on. It causes confusion.

O.S. in brackets after a character's name means 'OFFSCREEN'. It indicates that the character is physically present in the scene but can only be heard onscreen. V.O. after a character's name means VOICEOVER and indicates that that character is not present in the scene but can be heard either by means of an electro-mechanical device such as a phone, radio or loudspeaker, or in narration over the scene. This is a commonly used device in film noir and is also used to allow characters to express their thoughts and intentions on screen, e.g. Sheen's Captain Willard in *Apocalypse Now*.

DIALOGUE

Dialogue is written immediately after the character's name and starts 2.5 inches from the left side of the page with each line 3.5 inches wide on average. Expert opinion varies on this depending on the literary source or the type of screenplay formatter used but it always ranges between three and four inches wide per line. I will discuss dialogue in depth in a separate chapter.

PARENTHETICALS

These are the little bracketed pieces of personal direction that occasionally follow an actor's name and precede his or her dialogue. They may also be inserted into the middle of a piece of dialogue but never after it. Once nicknamed 'wrylies' because of the commonly used direction (wryly) these were used to indicate to actors how they should emote while delivering the associated piece of dialogue.

Actors hate 'wrylies' and most score them out before reading a script. It's argued that they serve no purpose, as the desired emotion should be obvious from the context of the scene and the character's mood. If not, the writer should revisit the script and rewrite it until it is clear. Don't use wrylies as a crutch for weak writing. Let the actors do their job. Leave room for them and let them bring their talent to the piece.

Use parentheticals sparsely and only as a last resort if there is a real and unavoidable risk of confusion. Nowadays, they are primarily used to describe little bits of action that occur within the dialogue, for example:

                         JOHN
                      (cocks gun)
                   Relax, take a seat.

It can include things like (slams door), (climbs stairs), (lights cigarette) and so on. It saves having to write out a separate line of action, which would then break up and disrupt the dialogue. However, don't overdo this either in frequency or word length. Parentheticals are also used to indicate who the actor is speaking to if there's more than one character present in the scene, for example:

> Joe
> (to Mary)
> What do you think?

FLASHBACKS

Flashbacks are introduced by writing FLASHBACK in capitals, left aligned, followed by the scene heading for the flashback and its story. Then, on returning to the story's present, write BACK TO THE PRESENT in capitals, left aligned, and the new scene heading of the story as it continues in the present of the story. Flashbacks should only be used if they advance the story in some dramatic way and should not be used merely for exposition or to reveal backstory. If done badly, flashbacks can slow the story and distract from it. Flashbacks are, however, commonly used in some movie genres such as film noir and many successful movies have used them. However, it has very limited use in a short screenplay simply because there is not enough time to use it correctly. How do you jump between the present and past in something that has very little time even to tell a story in the present?

TRANSITIONS

Transitions such as CUT TO and DISSOLVE are generally no longer used when writing a writer's draft script. It's argued that they're an unnecessary editing instruction as each new scene heading indicates the use of a cut anyway.

Don't write things such as SMASH CUT or CRASH CUT as they're screenwriting nonsense. All cuts are one frame long and cannot happen any faster. The writer is really trying to indicate that he wants the transition to generate a shock response in the audience. The context and content of the scene itself should make this clear. Ultimately the director will decide how it's cut. Shock is often created by using a sudden blast of noise or sound.

Generally writers no longer use CONTD for 'continued' at the top and bottom of a page or after a character's name when his or her dialogue is broken by a line of action. It breaks the flow of reading and adds unnecessary text to the page.

SUPER, INSERT TITLE

If you want to superimpose a title on screen such as AUSCHWITZ 1944 or ROME, 59BC then add SUPER or INSERT TITLE in capitals, left aligned and follow it with whatever you want to insert on screen. This is not the same as subtitles.

INTERCUT

If you want to cut between characters speaking at once in two different locations, for example having a two-way phone conversation, write INTERCUT in capitals in the scene heading then the two locations and the fact that it's a phone conversation in the action line. Alternatively, you can show the same thing with one character heard only as a voiceover. If the scene is being played out with one character inside a building, car or some interior location and another outside, perhaps looking in through an open window, leaning against a car door or whatever, indicate it by using INT/EXT followed by the locations and scene set-up in the action line.

SOUND

It's now becoming increasingly common for writers to capitalise sound effects for emphasis – a device copied from shooting-script sound cues – for example, the cannon BLASTS, the bell RINGS, the tyres SCREECH. Again, don't overdo it as it can become annoying to read.

Do not suggest title music, songs or a music soundtrack as this is the director and music supervisor's job. A specific piece of music should only be mentioned by name if it plays a significant role in the plot, e.g. *Sea of Love* or 'As Time Goes By' in *Casablanca*. Obtaining music rights and clearance is a legal minefield for filmmakers and expensive. In reality, this is well beyond the scope of most short screenplays. However, even in shorts, music plays a part and often causes problems. Music generates mood and influences emotion and can really add to a short film; however, the rights and clearances can be tortuous. The writer should avoid scripting scenes where music copyright will become an issue; for example, don't have Dave and Samantha meet at a Take That concert or write a script about a band or musician unless you're certain you have the rights to use their music.

PRESENTATION

Screenplays are always written on one side of white A4 or US Letter paper. Always use a good printer and black ink if sending a hard copy. Always write the script in the present tense. Don't number scenes or include camera angles and technical directions. Write the page number at the top right of the page but do not include it on the first page. Page one is the page with the first scene on it, not the title page.

Screenplays are always three-hole punched – an American standard – and held together with paper clips known as Brads inserted in the top and bottom holes only. Temporary clips like these are used so that script pages can be separated and photocopied. Some companies in the UK and Europe will accept other types of binding but it must not be permanent. Permanent binding will mark you out as an amateur. Stick to the standard, it's easier.

The title page and back cover are plain white card stock usually around 240gms in weight. The title page contains 'title by your name' centred with your name and contact details and the name and contact details of your agent if you have one in the bottom-left and right-hand corners. Don't forget your contact details if you want someone to get back to you!

Do not include fancy artwork, photos, coloured covers, permanent binding, cast lists, attachments or gimmicks of any kind in a screenplay.

Never write 'copyright of' or dates and draft numbers on a writer's draft. Paranoia about script ownership puts professionals off. Dates and draft numbers are only for use on scripts that have been purchased and put into development by a production company or for shooting scripts.

9. BEGINNINGS, MIDDLES AND ENDS

Every story has a beginning, middle and an end. Greek philosopher Aristotle was the first to document this self-evident fact in his book, *Poetics*. Over time this idea evolved and became known in screenwriting circles as the Three-Act Structure or paradigm as popularised in the 1980s by Hollywood screenwriting guru, Syd Field.

Syd Field's three-act paradigm has often been criticised as being too formulaic, with each act, turning point and the inciting incident being allocated a specific position within the screenplay. The three acts were allocated an approximate 25 per cent/50 per cent/25 per cent share of screenplay time. Syd Field also called his three acts the 'set-up', 'confrontation' and 'resolution'. This description is more helpful when it comes to writing and understanding short-film screenplays. We are, of course, referring to the longer dramatic short films, especially those that fall within the 10- to 25-minute range.

Short screenplays do indeed have set-ups, confrontations and resolutions but they do not adhere to Syd Field's prescriptive 25/50/25 split. The length of each act can vary substantially depending on the nature of the story being told. There is no prescriptive allocation of time, merely that they do need to be set up, do have a middle with confrontation, conflict and complications, and do indeed need to bring it all together in an emotionally charged climax that satisfactorily resolves the story.

THE BEGINNING: SET-UP AND HOOK

In short screenplays and films it is critical to begin fast and hook the reader and viewer in the first few minutes. I cannot emphasise this enough. Most short films fly or die in that crucial first three or four minutes. It's well known that in the feature film world the first 10 pages of a screenplay are crucial. If it fails to grab the reader's attention in that time it is typically rejected. The film festival equivalent of this is what is known as the 'four-minute rule'. Most significant festivals receive countless hundreds, if not thousands, of entries to their competitions. Selection panels view 50, 60 or more a day. A film that fails to hook the selectors and programmers' interest in that crucial four minutes is unlikely to be watched in full or selected for screening. It's a hard fact of life in the short-film world. If your beginning and set-up are weak your story is likely to be too.

A strong opening is crucial to success. I have seen many, many short films fail abysmally because of long, slow, moody openings where the character did nothing of interest, there was no hook and much time was wasted on pointless walking about, wake-up and washing sequences, staring into mirrors or out bus windows and so on. You must be able to set your story up quickly. Start fast, hook the viewer, introduce your protagonist and his problem and get to the heart of the story straightaway. Generally, moody slow burns do not work well in shorts. First impressions count, especially with the professionals. There's no time in a short screenplay for visual waffle.

Successful beginnings often pack a remarkable amount into a very short space of time, often only a couple of minutes. The things you need to set up very much depend on your unique story, its subject matter and scope. The best way to open your screenplay is to know your ending so you can work towards it, planting the right cues, orchestrating the required conflict and so on. It's my belief that you should never begin to write until you know your screenplay's end. It may change as you write but you need to have a relatively clear idea where you're going. In fact, beginning with the end as a prologue can be a very effective way to hook interest. Features regularly do this. *Citizen Kane* opened with Kane's death and his infamous last word 'Rosebud' then moved to tell the story of his life.

When a short film begins the audience wants to know immediately who it's following and what the story is about. They're waiting eagerly for the story, hot with anticipation and will use whatever information you give them in those first few opening minutes to try and figure it all out. Generally, the beginning needs to include most, if not all, of the following to get the story going:

- The set-up
- A hook
- A fast opening
- An inciting incident, catalyst or 'push' – what starts the story moving?
- Introduce the protagonist – what does he or she want?
- Introduce his problem, dilemma, predicament
- Introduce the antagonist and his want. Why does he oppose the protagonist?
- Introduce the story's world – its location, setting, time
- What kind of story is it? Its tone, style, genre
- Raise a central question – is there a premise or theme?
- Indicate what's at stake for the protagonist
- Introduce the key conflict and get the action moving

This may seem like a lot but much of it can be done simultaneously. A strong opening image alone can tell us much about the story's world as the eye can take in so much information from a single, well-selected image and the appearance of the character and location. A title card can sometimes be used but be brief – we want to see a story not read it. Audiences typically identify with, and focus their attention on, the first significant character they see so always introduce the protagonist first. If possible, create a memorable entrance for him or her and thrust him immediately into the heart of the story.

Short films should always begin as close to the action as possible. Begin with the story already in motion. In a short film the inciting incident should occur as close to the start as possible; in fact, begin with it if you can. It is the catalyst or 'push' that sets the story in motion. It should quickly introduce the character's problem, predicament or dilemma and indicate what he wants and what's at stake. It's also important to introduce the antagonist or antagonistic force early on so the other side of the equation is set up as well.

The antagonist should be a strong, compelling character in his or her own right with goals of their own, in opposition to the protagonist. The opening should also raise the central question of the story and perhaps hint at a theme. What's your story about? Is it love, survival, justice, righting a wrong, doing the right thing, revenge, becoming a man, protecting those you love, dignity, standing up for yourself, glory and success, what?

All good shorts contain a hook; indeed, I'd argue it's essential. A hook catches something and in screenwriting it catches the viewer and reader's attention and interest. It draws you in, arouses your curiosity and makes you want to know – what happens next? The hook needs to be compelling, well thought out and needs to grab the audience in those vital opening minutes. The hook can be simple and subtle. It doesn't have to be a murder or a dramatic fistfight. What matters is that it is compelling and instantly grabs our attention. It can be based on the character, an incident, a line of dialogue, the problem, a threat, a question, something in an opening voiceover, a striking image, the situation itself, anything. Just make sure you have one.

THE MIDDLE

The middle is the core of your story. It is where the plot thickens and the bulk of the dramatic action and conflict plays out. It develops the story, shows your character in action struggling against serious obstacles, fighting for what he wants against a powerful antagonist who fights back hard. The middle is where much of the battle is won or lost. It prepares the way for the hero's triumph – or defeat – at the end of the story. It sets up the final confrontation and climax. The greatest obstacle or set back for the protagonist should occur towards the end of the middle act – the darkest hour comes before the dawn.

The problem for short screenplays is that time is limited. In the middle the protagonist has only enough time to deal with one or maybe two obstacles at most. The conflict cannot become too complicated. Nevertheless this central period of conflict should still pack a punch. It should be intense, full of rising tension and suspense and promise a dramatic end to the story. It is also possible to imply dramatic developments offscreen, developments that impact on the character and his or her struggle. The saying 'out of the frying pan into the fire' should be the motto of the middle act at least as far as the protagonist is concerned. The struggle must become progressively more difficult for him or her. Other key points to keep in mind for the middle act are:

- Pace – don't let it sag. This is a common mid-act problem.
- Keep the characters active, energetic, engaged and on the move.
- Raise the stakes for both sides of the conflict.
- Don't get sidetracked into a subplot or secondary issue.
- Rising tension – keep building suspense, urgency and anticipation.
- Keep the antagonist strong for the final battle.
- Make life hell for the protagonist but give him the strength to somehow see it through to the end.
- Use surprise twists, setbacks or reversals where appropriate to add difficulty, uncertainty and tension.

False resolutions can also be used in the middle to add interest. The protagonist appears to defeat the antagonist and win what he was seeking but then discovers that the antagonist – or one of his allies – returns and that a much greater problem lay hidden behind him. Achieving his initial goal didn't really give him what he wanted. Now he has to resume his fight to solve this bigger problem and win. It adds an extra dimension to the story. The end of the middle takes us to the threshold of the final confrontation: the climax.

THE END

A short-screenplay ending can be open or closed, up or down, happy or sad, positive or negative, or even ambiguous, but whatever it is it must be worth the wait. You can do almost anything in a short but the most satisfactory endings from the audience's point of view are usually closed endings. There is a definite resolution. We know how it ended and nothing is left unsaid or unresolved. It should have meaning and an emotional impact and leave us thinking as we leave the cinema. This will depend not only on how well you've crafted your story but also the subject matter. A good comedy might just leave us feeling happy and entertained. In fact, every short should leave us feeling we've been entertained regardless of its content. Generally there's more room for creativity, originality and unpredictability in the ending of a short film than there is in a commercial feature. Down endings can be risky in a feature but work well in a short.

Avoid implausible, silly, unlikely and contrived endings or ones based on coincidence and the sudden appearance of some previously unmentioned skill or talent that somehow saves the day. Don't use coincidence, chance or luck to sidestep plot problems. Audiences hate 'deus ex machina' endings. It creates enormous dissatisfaction.

Deus Ex Machina – literally 'a god from the machine' – was an ending common in Greek drama. At the end of a play an actor representing one of the gods would be lowered onto the stage on a wooden platform – the machine. He or she would pass judgement on the various characters in the story and decide the ending. The ending came from the gods not the story. In Ancient Greece the gods decided everything among mortals. Greek audiences generally accepted that.

Today, however, endings must develop logically and plausibly out of the events in the story. You must stick to the truth of your story and have a natural honest ending that makes sense to the audience, one that is feasible within the world of the story you've created. Stay true to your story, plot, characters and their struggle. The end must reflect the set-up and answer the central question of the story. It must also resolve any major outstanding issues and pay off anything you've planted earlier in the story. Respect your audience's intelligence.

CLIMAX, RESOLUTION, REVELATION

The climax is the most intense final scene. It's the decisive point of the story and plot. It is usually preceded by a crisis for the protagonist. The climax will have both the protagonist and antagonist present. It tends to be active, external, dramatic and emotional and is the point at which the physical and emotional stakes and suspense reach their highest point. It brings about absolute and irreversible change for the characters. Their world will never be the same again. It's full of meaning and emotion and is also your last chance to say what you want as regards the story's theme.

The end can be spectacular, full of dramatic action and conflict, or it can be quiet and momentous, full of emotion, revelation and insight. Either way it must be emotionally satisfying. Many short films end very effectively, not with fists, guns or bangs, but with a dramatic revelation and insight. The climax then becomes a verbal confrontation between the characters during which one of the characters reveals – or is forced to reveal – startling new information that sheds new light on the story and the characters' struggle within it. Relationship dramas often end this way. The revelation acts as a surprise, a twist that gives us new insight into the story. Twists are typically revelation endings. In *The Sixth Sense* it's revealed that Bruce Willis's character is actually dead. It's a revelation for both the character and the audience. The twists in *The Crying Game*, *The Usual Suspects* and *Chinatown* were all dramatic revelations as well.

Twist endings work well and are popular in short film but they can also be a cliché. Don't twist for twist's sake. Don't try to be too clever, as a bad or implausible twist can backfire enormously. Twists need to be original, fresh, imaginative and well hidden. If the audience sees it coming it will fail. Endings with psychopathic killers who come back to life are so common now we expect it as a matter of course. Twists need to be good, well hidden and credible.

Twists and suspense do not tend to go together well. Suspense requires that the audience possesses certain information whereas twists have to be hidden until the last possible moment if they're to be effective. The 1963 Oscar winner *La Rivière du Hibou* or *An Occurrence at Owl Creek Bridge* contains a classic twist ending. Based on Ambrose Bierce's classic American Civil War short story of the same name, this French-made, 28-minute, black-and-white short is also an example of a film that uses very little dialogue.

Revelations can also work earlier in the ending. A judiciously placed revelation can free the protagonist from some previous constraint. The resulting insight spurs him on to confront his nemesis with renewed vigour in the final showdown. Revelations during or at the start of a showdown can also intensify the final battle between the opponents. For example, the antagonist reveals something to the protagonist that angers or infuriates him and increases his determination to win. Revelation can play numerous roles in a screenplay.

RESOLUTION

Resolution usually follows the climax in most feature films. It resolves any outstanding questions and typically shows the hero relaxing, adjusting to his new world and enjoying the fruits of his success. However, in short films, there's seldom much time for resolution scenes. It is often better to end on the dramatic climax, to go out on the 'bang' as it were.

Resolutions can be anti-climactic and reduce the impact of the climax unless they give us one last revelation and insight. If at that stage you still have a lot that needs resolving it's advisable to revisit your set-up and story and either reduce the number of these issues or find a way to resolve them before or during the climax itself. Don't drag the resolution out in a short film. It's more emotionally satisfying to end on the dramatic 'bang' of the climax if you can.

Finally, when your screenplay is complete, it's a good idea to work backwards through your script to check that everything was set up right. Does everything lead plausibly to the ending you've written? Are there any inconsistencies, plot holes, unnecessary scenes, dialogue or actions? Have you planted everything you need and paid it all off? Does it all fit together and flow logically? Delete anything you don't now need. Now pause and reconsider. Now that you know your whole story and have it all written, is there a better ending? Can you enhance it? Make it more dramatic? Is it the best, most emotionally satisfying way to end?

William Goldman advised, 'Give the audience what they want but not the way they expected.' Robert McKee agreed: 'Give the audience the experience we've promised but not in the way it expects.' François Trauffaut adds, 'Great endings are a combination of spectacle and truth.' In short, end well, and in the words of those old showbiz veterans, 'Leave 'em wanting more.'

10. CHARACTERS, GOALS AND MOTIVATION

Films are about people and audiences identify with people and their struggles. Characters are central to any story; indeed they carry the story and drive it to its climax. Without them there is no story. We experience the story through a character we identify or empathise with so characters need to be believable, fully rounded, three-dimensional people, not flat, one-dimensional stereotypes and clichés. They have to have goals, desires, wants and needs and specific objectives to pursue, whether they're the hero, the villain or, indeed, some secondary character. In short, a character we empathise with wants something so badly he'll do anything to get it and we're hooked.

How do you create this character? How do you do all this when you only have limited time available in a short screenplay? You may only have enough time to hint at some key elements of a character, enough for the audience to fill in the blanks and get a sense of something deeper. In the screenplay you must communicate as much as possible about the character in as few words as possible.

Short films tend to be very character centred because there's so little time to use many of the other storytelling techniques available to feature filmmakers. The power or strength of the characters must compensate for the practical, technical, budgetary and narrative limitations of the short form and carry the story.

The lack of a transformational arc is one significant difference from feature films. The character has little or no time to change significantly except for perhaps a dramatic revelation or sudden insight into his condition at the end. Interestingly, in some shorts the protagonist actually causes other characters to change while he himself remains relatively unchanged.

Characters should have inner and outer dimensions, flaws, secrets and recognisable personality traits. Even the villains should have some likeable and humanising traits. Characters need to be highly motivated and face real challenges and dilemmas. Character is realised through action and the decisions the character takes when confronted by seemingly impossible problems. Writing credible characters takes time and is one of the most difficult tasks facing the screenwriter. It's an enormous subject within screenwriting and the following are just some key points to consider.

CHARACTER TYPES

In a short screenplay the focus is usually on just two main characters – the protagonist and antagonist. The protagonist or hero drives the story and we follow him or her in their pursuit of their goal. The antagonist opposes the protagonist and obstructs his attempts to achieve what he wants. The antagonist doesn't have to be bad, evil or a villain – he could be a perfectly decent character who is simply a love rival, for example. He's an antagonist because he competes with the protagonist for the girl's attentions. The antagonist should be as strong and well crafted as the protagonist. Strong, equally matched opponents produce more interesting conflict. In many short films there's only a protagonist and the role of the antagonist is filled by a problem he has to solve. Overcoming the problem is his goal.

A range of different types of character can play the role of a secondary character. They can be allies and support characters on either side of the conflict or fulfil roles such as the romance character – the love interest. The confidant is a buddy type character in whom the protagonist confides his fears, doubts, hopes and wants. He may also discuss his intentions or plan of action. The confidant allows the protagonist to externalise his thoughts and feelings but beware of using him for 'on the nose' exposition. A similar 'sidekick' character can exist on the antagonist's side. The catalyst character can be used to trigger conflict or set up a problem. The mentor acts as an adviser giving advice to the hero. He can also be a confidant.

Minor characters can be used to populate scenes to make them appear more authentic or they can play other roles such as delivering messages, adding humour or flavour to a scene, or dying to show the consequences of failure. In a short screenplay characters should generally be kept to a minimum because multiple actors increase the cost of the short film. So how do we build a character?

BIOGRAPHY AND BACKSTORY

We are all shaped by our upbringing and past; so, too, are our characters. They all have to come from somewhere. Each has a life before the story begins and each will have a biography and a backstory. Creating a biography and backstory for your character is an excellent way to get to know your character even though you'll probably use less than ten per cent of it in your story. This process is very helpful in developing and creating a fully rounded, three-dimensional character and can also spark ideas for dramatic incidents within your story. You need to know your character inside and out to be able to write their story. Some writers have said that they found their characters coming to life inside their heads when they did this. It made it easier to understand how they'd behave, react, speak, make decisions and relate to other characters in the story.

The biography includes physical things such as age, gender, ethnic identity, birthplace, physical attributes and characteristics, grooming and so on. Social, cultural, economic and environmental factors can include such things as class, education, occupation, family background and circumstances, nationality, political or religious beliefs and so on. Psychological factors will include such things as the character's morality, sexual behaviour, attitudes, temperament, inhibitions, neuroses, complexes or obsessions, flaws, phobias, intelligence, degree of introversion or extroversion and so on. Don't go overboard with detail and keep it in perspective. Identifying key moments and influences in your character's life can be extremely useful.

The character's backstory deals more specifically with events in the recent past that led directly to the character's involvement in the story. The backstory tells us about events preceding the story. It helps us to understand how and why the character came to be involved in the story. Both biography and backstory will help you understand your character and his or her motives in the story. Discovering key dramatic moments in the backstory can lay the basis for dramatic revelations later on.

If there's an air of mystery audiences will also want to know backstory. It arouses their curiosity and involves them. However, while backstory and biography informs our, the writer's, understanding of the character we must use other techniques to reveal the character on the page.

FIRST IMPRESSIONS

We all tend to judge people by first impressions. Meeting a character for the first time on screen is no different. You can tell the audience a lot about your character by how you present him or her to them in terms of their physical appearance, posture, clothing, grooming, habits, mannerisms and mode of speech. How do they speak? Are they polite and formal, slow and deliberate, intense and edgy, profane, mocking, quiet and shy, arrogant and aggressive? Create an interesting entrance for them. Set them in an interesting location or create an opening scene that tells us something about their character. Better still; introduce them by showing them in action, actively pursuing their goal and already in conflict with the antagonist.

NAME

Choose a name for your character carefully. Names and nicknames bring with them certain associations. We can use them to suggest or imply things about our character such as class, ethnic or cultural background, sexuality, social attitudes, self-image and so on. There is usually a story behind every name and nickname.

EMPATHY AND EMOTIONAL IDENTIFICATION

Why should the audience root for your character? The audience usually experiences the story by following the character they identify and emotionally connect with. They also tend to identify with the first main character they see on screen so you should generally introduce the protagonist first. He or she will be the driving force of the story. How do we ensure that the audience emotionally engage with our lead character? There are several techniques that can be used to create emotional identification and empathy. Hollywood script consultant Karl Iglesias analysed these techniques in his excellent book *Writing for Emotional Impact*, which I'd highly recommend to all screenwriters. Karl suggested that we like or care about:

1. Characters we feel sorry for

2. Characters who possess humanising traits

3. Characters who possess qualities we admire

These attitudes and behaviours reflect the actual findings of social psychology, studies that examine the way we as human beings think and relate to one another in the real world. We transpose these emotional attitudes and perceptions onto characters we see onscreen and identify with them accordingly. We feel sorry for victims of injustice or hardship, people who are helpless and defenceless and who suffer undeserved maltreatment, brutality, misfortune and abuse, or suffer from some form of mental or physical handicap. We empathise with people who have been betrayed, abandoned, humiliated and embarrassed, people who are lonely, neglected, rejected, isolated or socially excluded, or those in great pain or danger. We identify and empathise with characters who find themselves in similar difficulties and who share the same kind of characteristics in a story. Putting a character in mortal jeopardy generates particularly strong feelings of empathy.

Similarly we like and admire people who show humanity and help the less fortunate, as well as those who are ethical, moral, unselfish, dependable, loyal, trustworthy, kind, generous, virtuous and loving, and so on. We tend to look up to those who risk their lives or even sacrifice themselves for others or those who suffer, fight or die for what we believe to be a just cause. Indeed, all societies regard such individuals as heroes, hold them in high esteem and present them with medals, awards and other honours to recognise their courage and selflessness.

We also tend to think well of people who are liked by children and animals. It's as if the child or animal perceives the inherent good in the person. If they think the person is good and trust them, we do too; at least that's the perception.

We also value and respect people who are courageous, powerful, charismatic, passionate, attractive, wise, intelligent and thoughtful, tenacious, successful, humorous, witty and determined in the face of adversity. We like underdogs who fight to better themselves as well as individuals who are talented, accomplished and masters in some field, whether it be sports, the arts, music, literature, business, or whatever.

If you can create situations in which your characters demonstrate any of the above qualities, behaviours or attributes then you will have created empathy and emotional connection. These are all aspects of real-life human behaviour that are well known to psychology. If you want to create real, believable, human characters then study the behaviour of real-life human beings. In my opinion, every writer should study and understand human psychology, especially social psychology and abnormal psychology. It's an absolute gold mine for screenwriters.

It's important to note that empathy does not mean that a character has to be likeable. Empathy means that you can understand and share the feelings of another, you can intellectually and emotionally identify with their emotional predicament. It does not mean that you necessarily like or want to be that person. You can empathise with Melvin Udall in *As Good As It Gets*, for example, without wanting to be him. He's not likeable but has empathetic qualities. Tony Soprano and Michael Corleone are ruthless mobsters yet they fascinate us as protagonists because we empathise with certain aspects of their character and personal situation.

REVEALING CHARACTER

How do you reveal character? Characters reveal their true selves by what they do, not what they say. To use those old clichés, talk is cheap and action speaks louder than words. A character is like an iceberg. Only the tip of his character is visible on the surface. We must create situations that force the character's true self out into the open.

The actions that the character takes and initiates reveal character. How does he or she act when faced with a dangerous or difficult situation? How does he deal with conflict? Famous playwright and dramatist Lajos Egri stated, 'Only in conflict do we reveal our true selves.' Character is revealed by the actions and decisions the character takes under stress, so put your character under extreme pressure in your story and see what he does.

What kind of decisions does he make when he faces an impossible dilemma and his back is to the wall? Choices are external and visual and usually lead to action. A character's decisions usually reflect their outlook, and attitudes, their values and beliefs, needs and wants. Choices have consequences for the character and affect his subsequent actions.

We may also learn about the character through dialogue but not necessarily his dialogue. How others speak of him or her when they're not present can tell us how others perceive them, who their real friends are and what they know of them. Additionally, contrasting what the character says with what we already know about them – the subtext – can also reveal much about their character, integrity, attitudes, and so on. Are they lying, cheating, deceiving, evading, or being honest and telling the truth? We can also contrast the character with other characters, their behaviours and actions and see what that reveals. We learn most about a character through action. The protagonist must always be an active character.

CHARACTER FLAWS

Perfect characters are unreal. Real people have inner flaws, fears and secrets, weaknesses and hang-ups, which play a significant part in their external attitudes and behaviours. Believable characters need to be the same. They have to have an imperfection, a hole in their inner soul. Characters often develop interesting defence mechanisms to hide these imperfections and present their best side to the world, or at least the image they want. Coming to terms with, and overcoming, inner flaws and weaknesses is often an essential part of the character's growth and psychological development. Unfortunately, in a short film there's often little time to develop this in depth unless we focus solely on a key moment of decision.

Another useful insight is to ask what is the character's darkest secret or greatest fear? What would he most fear being revealed? If you can find a way to exploit and externalise such inner fears it can create powerful conflicts for the character. It can explain why he acts as he does in certain situations. It creates interesting character contradictions and intriguing drama.

GOALS

What does the character want? How badly does he want it and what will he do to get it? A goal is a clearly defined objective that a character pursues. A goal should be strong enough to credibly generate the action and conflict in the story. The audience needs to believe that the character really wants to achieve this goal and is willing to sacrifice all to get it. A goal cannot be shared – there must be only one winner. Compromise is not an option in a dramatic story.

Some things a character wants; some things he needs. What a character wants and needs may be two very different things. The character may not even be able to articulate his need, as it may be deeply repressed and subconscious. There can be conflict between the two. In some stories characters discover in the climax that they didn't really need what they wanted. For example, they pursue fame and fortune only to discover that what they really wanted all along was love. Sometimes they gain what they wanted only to lose the one they love. The loss brings realisation.

The character's goal needs to be very specific. It needs to be simple and clear, something that the audience can easily follow and understand.

A goal that is too vague or abstract leads to character choices and actions that are vague and confused. It does little to encourage audience involvement. Sweeping goals like love, friendship and world peace are too vague to hold the attention of an audience. Specificity creates focus. If you want the audience to be on your character's side, you need a strong, clear reason for it. A character without a clear objective will frustrate. Audiences don't like characters who are weak and indecisive or who flounder in times of crisis. A goal on its own is not enough; the character also needs the will to go after it. He must have the will to succeed and be prepared to act.

MOTIVATION

In a short film the character's motivation to act must be strong, easy to identify, and his pursuit of his goal must be uncompromising and unrelenting. Why do people do what they do? Why does your character act? Why does he pursue a particular goal? What motivates him to risk all and suffer what he has to endure fighting against his antagonist? What prods the character to action?

Motivation is one of the most complex areas of human psychology and, of necessity, we can only touch briefly on it here. The very word 'motive' is related to motion. Motives compel a character to act for a reason. They act to achieve a goal, whether it be gaining something advantageous or preserving and protecting something precious. The individual may be motivated by a desire to be materially, physically, emotionally, intellectually or spiritually better off or he may act to preserve the material, physical, emotional, intellectual or spiritual 'property' that he already has. He may also act to advance or defend the interests of his family or some other social grouping that he belongs to or feels loyalty to and affinity with. A character's motivation can develop and grow over the course of the story.

A character's motives may be higher – love, honour, esteem, enlightenment, spiritual, scientific or intellectual advancement, sacrifice for the good of his fellow man – or they may be base – lust, greed, avarice, jealousy, power, selfishness, the seven deadly sins and so on. Abraham Maslow's ladder provides an interesting guide to human need and want. At its most basic level sits survival. Human beings need to be able to survive and so hunger, thirst, safety and security, shelter and warmth figure very high on the scale as motivators. Next we need love, companionship, belonging and self-respect. Love, sex and procreation, family and the protection of those we care for are powerful motivators. The higher we move up this ladder the more we move into the areas of self-esteem, intellectual advancement, discovery and enlightenment and higher spiritual values of self-actualisation.

How do we know what a character's motives are? They need to be externalised. They need to be embodied or enacted visually in some way. It may be made clear through dialogue, comments the character or others in the story make, or through actions and decisions. The character may verbalise his thoughts, fears, intentions and wishes, whatever, in a voiceover at some point, or he can reveal them through a confidant or buddy character to whom he confides his feelings, fears, wishes and intentions.

Trying to figure out what a character's true motives are engages an audience's curiosity and can really stimulate interest. However, for this approach to work, the character's actions, dialogue and subtext have to be really intriguing. His true motives are typically revealed at the climax. Don't prolong the revelation as the audience can become frustrated if it has to wait too long to find out.

In conclusion, in your short screenplay you must create a believable, three-dimensional protagonist who is strongly motivated to act in pursuit of a clearly defined goal against an equally well-crafted antagonist who opposes him. The character reveals his true self through the choices he makes and the way he acts during the escalating conflict. He may have to overcome his own inner demons and flaws before he's strong enough to defeat the antagonist. A well-drawn, multi-layered character can really make a short film.

11. CONFLICT, OBSTACLES AND STAKES

All drama is conflict. Without conflict there is no drama, no story and no screenplay. Conflict is the essence of great storytelling. It's the driving force that energises the characters and moves the story forward. It generates action and is integral to all narrative filmmaking. Conflict forces characters to make decisions, solve problems and act in pursuit of their goal. It forces them to reveal their true nature and drives their emotions and intentions out into the open. Without conflict they have nothing to do. Conflict galvanises audiences and ignites powerful emotions both on and offscreen. The sooner conflict erupts in your story, the sooner you will hook the reader and audience. If you can, you should open your story while your protagonist is locked in the middle of an ongoing conflict.

All great writers embrace conflict and confrontation even if we all shun it in our ordinary lives. Conflict lies at the heart of all great drama. You must study it, tune into it and use it if you want to write gripping and successful stories and screenplays.

WHAT IS CONFLICT?

At its simplest, conflict is a struggle between opposing forces. In its most basic form it leads to physical clashes, fights and combat between individuals, groups, armies, societies, nations. War is its most extreme form. However, conflict can also mean an opposition between ideas, interests, simultaneous but incompatible wishes, desires, drives, wants and needs. Conflict can occur without any physical violence or interaction taking place whatsoever. Conflict can exist on many different levels and for many different reasons. Conflict can be a dragon with many heads, each of which the hero may have to slay to achieve his goal.

Conflict can manifest itself in dialogue, in the character's actions and behaviour, in the subtext and interplay of secrets and hidden agendas, or it can be silent and show itself only in non-verbal cues and body language. It can be expressed in many different ways. It can be violent or non-violent, overt or covert, direct or indirect, openly stated or subtly implied.

In the most successful stories there will be multiple layers of conflict, but the story will revolve around one central or primary conflict, the one between the protagonist and antagonist. While battling the antagonist, the protagonist may also have to battle his own inner demons, fears and doubts – his inner psychological conflict – while also fighting with allies, friends or family who want him to hold back or follow some other course of action. He may also face obstacles such as the weather, environment, technological or transport problems and so on. He may even face preliminary or secondary attacks from allies and supporters of the antagonist. The antagonist, too, will have his own secondary conflicts to worry about.

Secondary conflicts can play an important, even critical, role in the resolution of the central conflict by weakening or strengthening one or other of the adversaries. They also add depth and colour to the story. The more conflict you can create in your story the better, but you must never lose sight of the central or core conflict.

It is important to ensure that the protagonist and antagonist are quite evenly matched and equal in strength. When both sides are strong the balance of power will oscillate between them. It creates extra tension and suspense because the outcome will always be in doubt. It rests on a knife-edge. If the opponents are mismatched then the outcome will never be in doubt and the story will be weak. Memorable villains are great for conflict and story.

TYPES OF CONFLICT

There can be internal and external, benign and malign, mental or physical, human and non-human conflicts. Ultimately, whatever the conflict, it needs to be externalised in some visual form so that we, the audience, can 'see' it on screen.

Internal conflicts occur when the character is riddled with doubt and struggling with some fear, phobia or difficult personality trait. He may have mental or emotional problems, inner demons, a destructive addiction or compulsion, or perhaps the ghosts of some past trauma, wrongdoing or indiscretion haunt him. Typically, resolving the inner conflict helps the protagonist gather the strength, determination and clarity of purpose needed to take on and defeat the antagonist. This inner turmoil needs to be externalised in some way if the audience is to see and enjoy it.

External conflicts are, of course, any kind of conflict between individual characters, groups, armies, societies, organisations, bureaucracy, governments, and so on, or when human beings struggle against some inanimate obstacle or antagonistic force such as the weather, environment, technology, geographical barriers, etc.

Benign conflicts are the kind of minor, non-destructive conflicts that occur between friends, workmates, lovers or families. They can add secondary interest but have little significance for the main story. Malign conflict is the kind that rips relationships apart and occurs when there's infidelity, distrust, abuse, rows about money, sex, children, addiction and so on. These serious conflicts occur when love and friendship are dead. Conflicts like these can be central to a story, e.g. *Kramer vs Kramer*, or have a major influence on the character's morale as he or she tries to overcome the antagonist.

Polarities and contrasts can be used to create conflict. Polarities of behaviour, values, interests and so on. Contrasts within a character can add depth to the character, e.g. the evil villain who loves pets is a clichéd version of this. Conflict should escalate as the story progresses in the face of increasing obstacles and rising stakes.

OBSTACLES

Obstacles create stumbling blocks for the protagonist. Obstacles prevent him from getting what he wants. He has to overcome them to continue towards his goal. The biggest and most powerful obstacle is, of course, the antagonist or villain who will do everything in his or her power to stop the protagonist. External obstacles can take the form of people, machines, groups or armies, the force of nature, terrain and the environment, weapons and so on.

Internal obstacles can take the form of a mental or emotional illness, a psychological wound in the form of a past trauma, an addiction or obsession, a character flaw, phobia or some other weakness or overriding passion that blinds him. Destructive emotions like jealousy, anger and rage can make him act rashly. With internal obstacles the character can become his own worst enemy and antagonist. He's at war with himself. The writer must always find a way to externalise such conflicts so the audience can see them and appreciate what's going on.

The hurdle race is one analogy for the protagonist's struggle against obstacles. He wears a backpack and as he runs his opponent increases the size of each successive hurdle and adds a brick to his backpack. If he falls he must get up again and try even harder. The only way he can win is through sheer grit, determination and by getting stronger all the time. The bricks and hurdles are the obstacles, stakes and weight of problems pressing down on him. The hurdles symbolise the physical, emotional and intellectual obstacles he must overcome.

Each obstacle that's encountered must be bigger than the one that went before and should also be different in nature so the hero has to employ a different strategy each time to overcome it. Variety maintains interest. Audiences become bored if the same obstacle is repeated over again, especially as the hero will know how to overcome it after the first time. Obstacles can be anything so long as they interfere with and block the protagonist and his pursuit of his goal. Much depends on the situation and context as well as the nature of the struggle. Let's look at an example using a sprained ankle.

THE SPRAINED ANKLE EXAMPLE

Obstacles that are trivial and meaningless in one situation can be critical in another. Let me demonstrate with a badly sprained ankle. It's not exactly life threatening so it shouldn't cause the protagonist any difficulty and hardly raises the stakes, or does it?

Imagine your story is a *Chariots of Fire*-type drama in which a young athlete has struggled against all sorts of personal and financial difficulties to train, compete and qualify for the Olympics. Now he's two days from competing for Gold, is everyone's favourite to win, and he sprains his ankle. The injury jeopardises everything he's worked so hard for. It's a personal disaster. How will he overcome this? Now a sprained ankle takes on enormous significance as an obstacle. It stands in the way of the hero achieving his goal.

But what if your story is one of boardroom politics and corruption. The protagonist is the owner of a major company facing a hostile takeover by a Gordon Gekko-type character. He sprains his ankle playing squash. This hardly matters when he's seated in a boardroom, being chauffeured around or working at a desk. It's more a nuisance than anything else. But let's say the antagonist stage-manages a boardroom coup. The critical meeting is to take place at 11 o'clock in the boardroom on the company's 30th floor. This meeting is going to be the showdown and climax of the story.

Now the protagonist arrives 15 minutes early for the meeting on the street with his injured ankle. When he enters the reception area he discovers that all the lifts are mysteriously out of action. He must climb 30 flights of stairs in 15 minutes. He has vital information that will totally neutralise the threat from Gekko but he can't use it if he's not there in time. All will be lost. Now suddenly his injured ankle is a major obstacle, so are the broken lifts and the 30 flights of stairs. By the 10th floor he's in pain, by the 20th he can barely stand, by the 25th the meeting is underway and he's in agony on his hands and knees. But just in the nick of time he staggers into the boardroom, helped by Joe the Janitor who found him on the 26th floor. Now we have drama, time pressure and a 'will he or won't he' conflict created by an injured ankle used in the right context. If we add information that the antagonist put the lifts out of action deliberately then we add subterfuge to the plot.

So you see: the kind of obstacle you create very much depends on the nature of the story you're telling and its context. Note, too, that neither of these conflicts involved physical violence yet both generate conflict and drama. The obstacle became significant and the conflict intensified because of what was at stake. Stakes matter in storytelling.

STAKES

What's at stake for the protagonist? How crucial is it? How dangerous is losing? How important is it that he wins? The stakes refer to two opposing things. First, what does the protagonist gain if he succeeds in his quest? Secondly, what does he stand to lose if he fails? The price of failure must be high; the reward for success must also be great. Both must be significant to make the struggle worthwhile. Win or lose, the stakes are high, with life and death being the highest of them all.

As a rule, the more crucial the goal, the higher the stakes tend to be. The higher the stakes, the greater will be the tension, suspense and conflict and the more interesting the story. The stakes must always be very significant within the terms of the story and worthy of the protagonist's efforts. The audience has to feel that the protagonist's goal is worthwhile and we need to care about whatever is at stake. A parent trying to save the life of his kidnapped child, yes; a parent trying to save his prize pumpkin from rodents, no! We have to care about the character and his goal for the stakes to matter.

Raising the stakes is a term that comes from poker and is very apt for a high-conflict situation. The writer must find ways to make life more difficult for the protagonist as the story progresses. The cost of losing should increase, as should the value of winning. His struggle becomes progressively more complicated. To do this it's necessary to leave room to make matters worse. However, in a short film you may only have time to do this once.

The purpose of raising the stakes is to increase the pressure on the protagonist and intensify the tension, suspense and urgency. It can sometimes be useful to sacrifice a minor character at a key moment to demonstrate what's at stake if the antagonist succeeds. If possible, the stakes should rise progressively throughout the story towards the climax. You can also put more than one thing at stake.

What kind of things should you put at stake? It could be something tangible and valuable like the life of a loved one, wife, girlfriend or child. It could be some prized or treasured possession, huge wealth or one's whole livelihood. It could be survival, safety, security, freedom, or even one's very sanity or life. On the other hand it could be some higher goal – love, honour, self-esteem, freedom, loyalty to one's friends, group or nation, religious faith or some belief system or ideological viewpoint. The stakes may present a physical, emotional, mental or spiritual danger to the protagonist. It all depends on the story and the nature of the conflict.

Stakes play a crucial role in building anticipation, tension, suspense and dread. They are key to eliciting an emotional response from the audience. In conflict something always has to be at stake. Karl Iglesias calls it the dreadful alternative. The hero must achieve his goal or something dreadful will happen. The interplay of conflict, obstacles and rising stakes creates dramatic tension in your story and creates strong emotional interest and involvement on the part of the audience. Conflict is the heartbeat of your story. Fill your short screenplay with it on every level.

12. ELICITING EMOTION

Why do audiences go to the cinema? What's the attraction? Basically they go to enjoy an emotional experience. They go to a horror film to be horrified, a thriller to be thrilled, a comedy to laugh and so on. It's an emotional as well as a social experience. We choose which film we go to see on the basis of the emotions we expect to experience. We can release stored emotions and fears and enjoy emotional experiences that are missing from our lives or forbidden by society. Emotion is the glue that bonds us together. It energises our daily lives and influences the way we relate to other human beings.

A GYM FOR THE EMOTIONS

Screenwriting guru Richard Walter calls cinema 'a gymnasium for the senses'. It's the place we go to give our emotions a work out. He believes that human beings need to feel strong emotions to feel alive and that our survival depends on our ability to deal with intense, stressful and challenging emotions. Cinemas are a place where we can rehearse these feelings and learn to deal with the emotional pressures of the real world. It's a safe place to experience frightening and unfamiliar emotions.

Movies typically deal with the many threats to our daily lives such as crime, war, bad, mad or evil people, relationship problems and all the stresses of living in an unstable world. Some stories act as models for life. They allow us to explore our emotions and experience things that we probably couldn't endure in real life.

Short screenplays have more freedom to deal with difficult issues. They can tackle emotionally charged subjects in a much more radical or original way. There is more scope to challenge the emotions especially when dealing with a critical moment in a character's life. A well-scripted short film can deliver a short, intense burst of emotion.

Psychologists claim we find out who we are by comparing ourselves to other people. Watching characters in movies is one way we do this. It's argued that we project ourselves into films that emotionally engage us. We enrich our sense of self-worth by projecting ourselves onto the characters we admire and, for a time, feel that we share their positive traits, talents and attributes.

When we feel very strong emotions our bodies undergo certain physiological changes as a result of the release of adrenalin, endorphins and other hormones. These hormones affect our mood and stimulate feelings of pleasure or excitement. In general, watching a film is a positive emotional experience. It also helps us to escape from that other soul-destroying emotion, boredom, and the dreariness and tedium of our very ordinary lives. So, as a screenwriter, you need to figure out: how do I give my audience an emotional work out? How do I generate emotional heat and send them on a rollercoaster of emotions? How do I satisfy their desire to experience powerful emotions?

DELIVERING EMOTIONS

The screenwriter's job is to evoke emotion and give the audience an emotional experience. Screenwriting guru Karl Iglesias put it this way, 'Hollywood is in the emotion delivery business. It trades in emotions.' Michael Hauge agrees: 'Your primary goal as a screenwriter is to elicit an emotional response in your audience.' Richard Walter calls screenwriters 'traffickers in emotion'.

Master of suspense, Alfred Hitchcock, put it this way when interviewed during the making of *North by Northwest*: 'We're not making a movie, we're making an organ like in a church. We press this chord and the audience laughs, we press that chord and they gasp, we press these notes and they chuckle.' He was the organ player and each key was an emotion. It was his job as director to pick and play the right emotional chords at the right moment to achieve the desired emotional effect.

If you want to write a short screenplay and produce a successful short film then you must focus all your skill and attention on the emotional impact of what you're writing. You need to think about creating situations, scenarios and stories that elicit powerful emotional responses. Every successful film does just that.

WHICH AUDIENCE?

Your audience is not just the people watching your film; it is anyone who reads your screenplay. It might be the people you want to recruit to make the film or it might be a script reader or development executive in a funding organisation or production company that you're trying to persuade to support your film. It may even be a reader in a screenplay contest. If the reader laughs aloud at the funny bits, has tears silently rolling down their face at some sad moment, skips their dinner because they just can't wait to find out what happens next or is afraid to turn out the bedroom light after reading your horror script then you've done your job and elicited the desired emotional response.

WHOSE EMOTIONS?

It's essential to differentiate between the emotions of the characters in the story and the emotions of the audience watching them. You must focus your attention on the emotional impact of what's being shown on screen on the real human beings sitting in the audience or reading the screenplay. Don't make the mistake of writing emotions for the characters onscreen only, emotions that might not resonate with the audience. Your target is the audience. It's their emotions you want to influence. If the audience do not connect with your characters or their predicament they may not share the same emotions while watching. Just because a character feels sad doesn't mean we, the audience, will. We might be glad he's sad because we don't like him or are happy he's being punished for some wrongdoing.

Avoid having your characters express clichéd, exaggerated or melodramatic emotions that simply aren't real or believable. If we are to buy into the story, the emotions the characters portray on screen have to be credible and reflect human reality. Ultimately you want the audience to actively experience the emotion rather than just sitting back passively watching some character on screen experience it.

This is what separates great storytellers, screenwriters and filmmakers from the rest – their stories successfully elicit the desired emotional response. The audience leaves the cinema feeling satisfied and tells all their friends that it was a great movie. They do so because they enjoyed the emotional experience. Get to know the emotional mind of the audience. Screenwriting is all about creating a satisfying emotional experience.

EMOTIONALLY SATISFYING

Hollywood is often criticised for being obsessed with happy or upbeat endings. Some argue that this simply reflects the inherent optimism of the American people, others that it reflects box-office success. There are stories of endings being rewritten to make them upbeat even when this didn't fit the underlying truth of the story. It's important to note that emotionally satisfying does not mean the same thing as happy. A story does not have to end on a high note to be satisfying. Many great love stories were tragedies with sad endings – *Love Story*, *Romeo and Juliet*, *Wuthering Heights*, *The English Patient*, *Dr Zhivago* – yet audiences left feeling thoroughly satisfied emotionally.

Short films can do anything. Liberated from the pressure of box-office return you have the freedom to write up, down or open endings just so long as they're emotionally satisfying and consistent with the dynamics of your story. Don't make the mistake of assuming that you have to write a happy ending for your short screenplay to be an emotional success. If your story comes to the appropriate conclusion for that type of story we'll feel emotionally satisfied. We can enjoy the emotional experience of the character's journey as well.

Additionally, characters do not have to be nice people. Melvyn Udall, Michael Corleone, Tony Soprano, Hannibal Lecter or Norman Bates are hardly people you'd bring home to meet Mum yet we find their dangerous, self-destructive personalities fascinating and can't wait to see what they do next. They stir a different type of emotion; indeed, some argue they allow us to dance with the dark side of our emotions. Fascinating characters like these can make interesting subjects for a short screenplay.

HOW DO WE ELICIT EMOTION?

We create interest and excitement. Interest and excitement are the opposite of boredom and apathy – the worst things that an audience can feel.

Excitement on its own can be generated by spectacle, high-octane car chases, battle scenes, fights and pursuits, explosions and intense action sequences as in action adventures, thrillers and war films, but the problem with this is that it becomes boring if that's all there is. Excitement on its own is not enough. There has to be some underlying story to hold our interest and give it deeper meaning. Endless activity without meaning is superficial and ultimately emotionally unfulfilling. Furthermore, spectacle on that scale is generally not practical in a short film. If your short screenplay does contain spectacle on this scale you need to reconsider – where are you going to get the resources to realise your vision? Are you really writing a feature?

Interest is the bedrock, the emotion that all the others link to. If we can't generate interest nothing else will work. We elicit interest by creating emotional involvement and we do that by creating an empathetic character, someone we care for or otherwise connect with as discussed in an earlier chapter. We then create emotional involvement by building a meaningful emotional experience around that character as they make their way through the tangled web of story that we've woven for them. James Cameron created the Rose and Jack story to emotionally connect audiences with the predicament of people on board the *Titanic* as it sank.

EXPECTATIONS AND UNCERTAINTY

The key to generating emotional interest is expectation and uncertainty. First create expectations. These have to be meaningful expectations, not something routine like expecting to go to work or eating dinner when you come home. These have to be expectations that grow out of the protagonist's goal, his problem, his needs and wants, or perhaps some threat that he faces. Plans, stated intentions, conflict and foreshadowing can all be used to create expectation. We expect something to happen because of X, whatever X may be.

Next we add uncertainty and unpredictability. Expectations are linked to the future and the future is always uncertain. We worry about the future because we don't know what it'll bring. It's a human trait. The only certainty we have is that death awaits. When we don't know what is going to happen it generates curiosity. Curiosity is a powerful emotion that hooks our interest and attention. Human beings are innately curious. Every good story contains mystery so we're always curious to know what happens next. How does it all end?

ANTICIPATION

Expectations create anticipation. We anticipate that something will happen but because of uncertainty we don't know when it'll happen, if it will happen, how it will happen or whether it will have a positive or negative outcome. Once again the anticipation must relate to something significant or meaningful to the story and not just anticipation of something trivial, unimportant or routine. It must have some dramatic weight and mean something to the character and to us. Anticipation in turn is linked to a range of other emotions, each with different outcomes as follows:

- **Fear and Suspense** – the anticipation of danger

- **Worry, Anxiety or Concern** – the anticipation of loss or harm

- **Hope** – the anticipation of something pleasant

- **Dread** – the anticipation of something unpleasant

- **Tension** – anticipation delayed

- **Surprise** – something that was un-anticipated

Each of these can be used to generate emotional interest. We can fear for the safety of the character during each phase of his struggle. We hope that the hero wins, defeats the antagonist and gets what he deserves but we don't know for sure if he will because the future's unpredictable and uncertain. So we worry. We're plagued by doubt. The delay causes tension. The suspense and dread can be great if the stakes are very high. We fear our hero won't make it, the danger is so great and the odds so high.

SUSPENSE

Suspense is the strongest emotion we can create because it is intense, electrifying and can be prolonged for much of the story. Suspense hooks interest and emotional involvement like no other emotion. To create suspense we must dangle an uncertain outcome with high stakes in front of the character. High stakes suggest a high price for failure, perhaps even death or the loss of all we hold dear, but equally the reward for success is great. We can ratchet up the suspense as the story progresses by increasing the uncertainty and unpredictability, adding surprises, increasing the risks and taking the conflict to the extreme.

We hope the protagonist will survive. We hope he'll win but we're terrified he won't. We're on the edge of our seats. Intense suspense stimulates the release of 'fight or flight' hormones that literally put you on the edge of your seat. If you can create that level of emotional response you're onto a winner. The immediacy of film adds strength to the emotional response because it creates real feelings of fear. Fear is the most primal of emotions because of its link to the survival instinct. Fearing for the safety of a character adds greatly to the suspense.

SURPRISE, SUBTEXT AND OTHER TECHNIQUES

Predictability is the enemy of most of these tools. Adding surprise at the right moment is a useful way to increase the uncertainty and unpredictability of the situation. Surprises in the form of twists can shock us and totally change the dynamics of a story. Playing with the probability of an outcome is another way to manipulate expectations.

The subtext of a scene can generate anticipation and suspense and create dramatic irony. For example, it may reveal some danger lurking beneath the surface that the character isn't aware of. If he's walking into a trap it'll generate suspense. By manipulating the flow of information going to the audience, choosing what to conceal or reveal and when, we can heighten the audience's sense of anticipation, tension, suspense and uncertainty.

Another useful technique is to up the ante and raise the stakes for the protagonist at key moments. Put him in greater jeopardy. Sacrifice a minor or support character to demonstrate the price of failure. This can be a useful way to heighten tension and intensify the emotional impact of the character's predicament.

Foreshadow future events by planting something early in the screenplay that will pay off later in the story. For example, a character making a threat, someone seen loading a gun, a leaking brake pipe, anything that we might expect is going to return to haunt the hero and potentially affect the outcome of the story. It's important to ensure that every plant is paid off before the story closes. Failure to do so will cause audience dissatisfaction.

Tension can be a very uncomfortable emotion for the audience to endure if prolonged. It's always advisable to write in little moments of relief, a character joking, a little breather while they reflect or plan, whatever, to relieve the tension before ratcheting it up again.

Create tension and suspense by creating parallel and converging lines of action for the protagonist and antagonist then cross cut between them. Add deadlines and time pressures and increase the pace as they close in on each other. We know that when the two paths meet there will be fireworks. Ideally this should be at the climax.

In conclusion, when writing your short screenplay, it's essential to create an emotional experience for the reader and audience alike. Construct an empathetic character then create emotional interest by generating expectations and anticipation. Add as much uncertainty, unpredictability and doubt as you can, then put your character in jeopardy and raise the stakes. Use the various techniques and tools at your disposal to create curiosity, fear, anxiety, tension and suspense and you will succeed in giving the audience an emotional experience they'll enjoy. Never forget, it's all about emotions.

13. DIALOGUE

The first thing to say is, don't write any. You immediately exclaim in horror, what! Okay, I'm exaggerating for effect. Of course you will write dialogue, maybe even quite a lot, but the point is this: in short film, where possible, dialogue should be kept to the minimum. Some of the best short films I've seen tell their story almost entirely using strong, carefully selected and skilfully cut images.

There are several problems with dialogue in short screenplays. First, many beginning screenwriters are not good at writing dialogue yet seem to associate writing screenplays with writing endless pages of it. The end result is scene after scene of 'talking heads' rambling on and on with horrible, wooden 'on the nose' dialogue that completely turns the audience off. It tells the story rather than showing it.

Remember, your dialogue has to be delivered by actors. If you're struggling to find professional actors for your film the chances are you'll end up using less experienced ones whose dialogue delivery may lack credibility. If so, this only compounds the problem if your dialogue is already substandard.

Secondly, most writers watch a lot more television than they do film or indeed short film. Compared to film, television drama is 'talky' and dialogue heavy. Talking-heads shots are commonplace and characters spend a great deal of time telling each other the story. Inevitably this influences the way beginning writers write. Film prefers to tell its story with interesting imagery rather than words. By contrast, talking heads produce static shots that are not visually interesting or exciting. Much, of course, depends on the subject of the film. Some stories such as romantic comedies or courtroom dramas will depend heavily on dialogue while action adventure or war films, horror and thrillers have substantially less. This also applies to short film; the choice of subject matter will influence the dialogue – visuals balance. In general, successful short films and screenplays use less dialogue than television.

SUBTITLES

The principal outlet and audience for short films is the global film festival and competition circuit. If you want to screen your short film in the many non-English-speaking festivals around the world, especially those in Europe, you will need subtitles. Some of the most high-profile festivals require French, Spanish, Italian or German subtitles.

Dialogue-heavy shorts need extensive subtitling which adds to cost but, more importantly, distracts significantly from the film's visuals. If you spend all your time reading subtitles you're not watching the film and so miss 80–90 per cent of the cinematic experience. This can be a serious problem. I've watched fast-talking, dialogue-heavy, short films that had as many as three lines of subtitles appearing simultaneously on screen. It was impossible to keep up with the dialogue and follow what was going on. After several minutes it became so frustrating that I simply gave up watching. Hence, if you've written a dialogue-heavy screenplay that's shot in English, you may have no choice but to restrict yourself to screenings at English-speaking festivals to avoid subtitling. You must think about this when writing your short screenplay. What do you intend to do with your screenplay and film? What is your strategy? If you want to compete for major prizes abroad you will either need to reduce your dialogue or rethink your story. Having a film with little dialogue and strong visuals is more appealing to global audiences and festival programmers.

WHY SPEAK AT ALL?

Why do we use dialogue? What is its purpose? At the most basic level we're telling – or showing – a story about real people living in the real world, and real people talk. It's as basic as that. However, people talk in many different ways and for many different reasons. Our problem as screenwriters is capturing and reflecting that diversity and uniqueness and making it sound credible.

People talk to get something they want, to exchange information, to socialise and enjoy human contact with friends, family and loved ones, to do their jobs, to establish, manage and mediate relationships with other people, groups, organisations and the world around them. Talking helps to create and maintain emotional bonds with those we care about. In a screenplay the writer uses dialogue for a number of specific reasons:

- To communicate essential information to the other characters and, more importantly, to the reader and audience.

- To reveal character.

- To propel the story forward by instigating or advancing action or creating conflict.

- To establish and manipulate the mood and tone of the story or some part of it – a scene or sequence. A dramatic revelation can suddenly change the mood of the story.

- To create anticipation, expectation, tension and suspense or set up and foreshadow future incidents, problems, dilemmas and conflict.

- To entertain, especially if it's a comedy. Audiences and actors like clever wordplay and humour.

- To elicit an emotional response from the audience.

Dialogue in a screenplay must always have a purpose. Always get to the point quickly and cut the waffle. Avoid frilly or boring chit-chat or what I call ding-dong dialogue where characters chatter aimlessly about trivial and irrelevant things before getting to the point of the conversation. It wastes valuable story and script time. We don't want to hear about the weather or last night's game or whether you want sugar with your tea or about your mother's bad back unless it has a role to play in the story. For example, if we know there's a ticking bomb under the table then suddenly the aimless chatter takes on a whole new meaning. It now plays a dramatic part in creating tension and adding to the suspense.

WHOSE VOICE?

One of the biggest complaints from script readers about dialogue is that the characters all sound the same. They lack individuality. They all speak with one voice, the writer's voice. This is particularly common with beginning screenwriters. A useful reader's tip is to cover the names of the characters then read the dialogue and see if you can tell them apart. Can you tell who's speaking just from reading the dialogue? Characters need to be differentiated and show their individuality in the way they talk. After all, they're supposed to be unique individuals with their own identifiable personas.

Dialogue is always tied to character. It must remain true to the character throughout the script. It's essential that you really know your characters, inside and out, before you start to write their dialogue, and indeed even before you write the script. Then, when they start to 'talk', let them be who they are in the story. Some writers say that when they really know their characters they can hear them come to life and 'speak' inside their heads as they write. Others like to link their characters' voices and mode of speech to people they know. They can then imagine the character speaking with the voice of that person as they write their dialogue. Either way, it's essential that, when the character speaks, it's with their own distinct 'voice'.

INDIVIDUALITY IN DIALOGUE

Many things can determine how a character speaks – their social class, education, upbringing, background, age, gender, life experience, ethnic identity, status, occupation, intelligence, and so on. All exert an influence and need to be taken into account when writing their dialogue. Even the characters' casual conversation can be shaped by the story's milieu and the events of the time. For example, post 9/11 it wasn't unusual to hear characters in American television dramas making passing reference to the events and aftermath of 9/11. Adding a little piece of dialogue that has a contemporary relevance to the story's setting can add authenticity to the drama but it can date it as well so don't overdo it. In general, a character's dialogue must be consistent with the following:

- Character's present circumstances, i.e. rich or poor, prison or palace, war zone or space station, elderly or teenage.

- Ethnic, cultural or religious background.

- Geographical background, i.e. urban or rural, New Yorker or Texan, Londoner or Parisian, Nigerian or Australian.

- Age – vocabulary, syntax and attitudes change with age. A five-year-old will speak very differently from a 15-year-old or 75-year-old. An elderly person's attitudes, speech patterns and vocabulary will have been shaped in a very different era.

- Time period – Tudor England, Ancient Rome, the swinging 'sixties, contemporary USA, planet 431 in the year AD 2480.

- Story location – Arctic, Saharan Africa, Europe, Asia, a remote village or busy city centre, military base or prison camp, steelworks or convent, Stalingrad or Pompeii.

- Life experience. For example, traumatic events can change an individual's personality and attitude to life, their relationships and the way they speak. A woman or child who has been the victim of some terrible sex crime may be very nervous or repressed near someone who resembles the perpetrator. They may have difficulties speaking and relating to people. The pain and anger of a refugee whose family have been massacred in some distant warzone will be reflected in their dialogue. Privilege and wealth in childhood may have made a character arrogant, selfish, spoilt and demanding, with all of that reflected in their dialogue.

- Intelligence influences vocabulary and syntax.

- Personal flaws, fears and limitations can shape a character's psychology and change the way they speak.

- Disabilities, whether physical, mental or verbal.

- Confidence levels – introvert or extrovert, humble or arrogant, shy loner or bombastic show-off.

- Occupation – beware stereotyping and the use of cliché. Remember there's an individual with a personality behind any uniform or authority role. Occupations tend to produce speech patterns marked by the use of jargon, technical vocabulary and phrases specific to that activity. Judicious use of carefully chosen jargon and slang can add authenticity to the dialogue but shouldn't be so obscure that the audience doesn't understand it.

- Attitude to life – pessimist or optimist, winner or loser, a victim or success.

- Historical events – living through or shaped by.

It's important to note that, as dialogue is always tied to the character, if the character changes in some significant way during your story, his or her dialogue will too. The two have to go hand in hand to be believable. For example, say the character was always cheerful, outgoing and friendly but then his family is butchered by enemy soldiers who he then pursues seeking revenge. His mood and personality will have changed and so too will his speech. The language of revenge will have replaced his initial cheerful, light-hearted dialogue. There may be intense anger and hatred or a brooding silence.

PROBLEMS WITH DIALOGUE

Dialogue problems can appear in a number of ways, some of which we've already discussed. The most common are as follows:

- Exposition

- On the nose

- Lack of individuality

- Anachronisms

- Character inconsistencies

- Writing in accents or dialect

- Clichés and stereotypes

- Too talky or wordy

- Too predictable

- Too stilted, formal or grammatically correct

- Flat, bland, wooden, lifeless

EXPOSITION

Exposition occurs when a character reveals information in a very direct way simply for the benefit of the audience or reader. It is often delivered in a clumsy way that doesn't fit the story. Sometimes so much information is spoon fed to the audience that it leaves them with no mystery, nothing to work out as they go along. Sometimes exposition is delivered by a minor character that drops into the story at some key moment, delivers his or her piece of exposition then disappears never to be heard of again. Badly delivered exposition can really spoil the credibility of a scene.

Characters never tell each other what they already know, why would they? Exposition needs to be subtle, clever and only reveal the minimum. Leave room for the audience to exercise their story brain. Audiences love trying to figure out what's going on. It keeps them actively engaged and interested in your story. We all like solving puzzles. Be clever about exposition, deliver it in small bites, disguise it in conflict, smuggle it in under the audience's radar by implying it in things characters say without using the actual words.

ON THE NOSE

Dialogue that is 'on the nose' is dialogue that is direct, to the point and means exactly what the speaker intended it to mean. It is word for word exactly what they're thinking or feeling at that moment. It is boring to listen to and leaves nothing for the audience to do. There's no subtext or hidden meaning. It's predictable, superficial and totally unrepresentative of how real people speak. For a start it leaves no room for that great human character trait – lying. In reality people often talk in riddles and often don't say what they really think for both good and bad reasons. People have hidden agendas and desires they keep hidden. Subtext is the opposite of 'on the nose'.

ANACHRONISMS AND JARGON

Anachronisms occur when words or phrases are used in the wrong period of history. For example, swear words, jargon, sexual references and slang used decades or even centuries before they were ever invented. I've heard 'dude' and 'man' used in films set in the early part of the nineteenth century and military slang and jargon that only appeared with the Vietnam War being used in films about the First and Second World Wars. Make sure that any jargon, slang or profanity you use actually belongs to the period you're writing about. Don't use technical terms and colloquialisms that no one understands outside of a very specific group. It will confuse the audience. Lack of individuality, character inconsistencies and being too talky we've discussed earlier.

ACCENTS AND DIALECT

Don't write in accents, dialect or foreign languages. Sometimes writers spell out accents and dialects phonetically thinking this will capture the character of the speaker more accurately. It has the opposite effect. It makes reading the script a struggle and makes it difficult to understand. It's a quick way to get your script binned. If you want to set up an accent or dialect, simply say so in the character's description then write their dialogue in plain English. The producer or casting director will then find an actor who can deliver the required accent. Alternatively, if the character appears only briefly in the story, simply put it in parentheticals after the character's name and before their dialogue, for example:

> JACKIE
> (Scottish accent)
> Right folks, drink up please!

If a character speaks a line of dialogue in a foreign language, again simply add it in parentheticals after the character's name and write whatever they say in English. The line will be translated and delivered appropriately during the shoot. The screenplay needs to be readable in the language in which it'll be produced. It's understood that characters in a story set in another country are speaking in their native tongue even though the actors speak in English; for example, the Nazis in *Schindler's List* spoke in English but we understood they were speaking in German. It's a filmmaking convention. The screenplay was written all in English.

Don't be predictable, avoid clichéd phrases and write dialogue that sparkles and leaps off the page. Flat, wooden dialogue or dialogue that is grammatically precise and obsessively correct is boring. Nobody except perhaps a stiff aristocrat speaks like that. In reality most people speak in short phrases. The exception is when a character is delivering a speech, sermon or lecture in a formal situation. Make sure their monologue is electrifying unless the plot requires them to be dull.

SUBTEXT

Subtext refers to the true meaning that lies hidden beneath the spoken word. The subtext reveals what the character is really thinking or feeling but not expressing in his or her dialogue. We deduce the true meaning from the context, the situation and our knowledge of the character and the story. We read between the lines, as it were, and elicit the true meaning. Subtext done well is the smartest type of dialogue there is. It's the opposite of 'on the nose' dialogue. Actors love to play it and it engages audiences intellectually as they try to figure out what's really going on. It implies subterfuge and deceit, hidden agendas, secret lives and undercurrents of conflict, invisible motives, duplicity and dishonesty, lies and fears, unspoken wants and desires, hidden stories, hidden lives, subplots and so much more.

Subtext is the way that people talk when they've something at stake emotionally. They fear to reveal what they really think because of the potential repercussions, which could include rejection by a love interest in a romantic comedy, execution by a tyrannical ruler if it's a political thriller or losing if they show their hand too early in a corporate power struggle.

You have to know what your character really thinks and feels before you can disguise it with subtext. Again, the dialogue originates with the character. There are many techniques that can be used for writing subtext. You can show an action, not dialogue, as a response to something or perhaps a meaningful silence. Characters can change the subject to sidestep and evade difficult questions or give an ambiguous and evasive answer using words that have double meanings. Characters can put on emotional masks – a false front or face – to hide their true feelings in difficult situations. You can use metaphors and symbolism, answer questions with questions or imply something without saying it.

Characters can 'talk to us' using the non-verbal cues of body language, looks, behaviours and actions, silences and what they choose not to say. Sometimes less is more. Physical actions or 'actor business' can be used to reveal a character's true feelings; for example, someone is playing cool and confident but the fact that his foot is tapping and he's fiddling constantly with a pen reveals his true nervousness and discomfort. Even the context can be used to show a meaning opposite to that expressed; for example, when Harry and Sally kiss at the end of *When Harry Met Sally*, Sally says with a smile, 'I hate you, Harry.'

OTHER ISSUES

The use of profanity and sexual swear words has become more common and acceptable in film nowadays but can still cause difficulties in some cultures or societies. On the one hand it may be a true representation of a character and accurately reflect the reality of certain situations, making the story more authentic and believable – who can forget Lee Ermey's fabulous drill sergeant in *Full Metal Jacket*? – but on the other it can be gratuitous, offensive and unnecessary. The writer needs to carefully consider whether it really belongs in his or her story and whether it'll be detrimental and distracting. It's a subjective value judgement. Some characters just don't sound real without it while others sound all wrong with it. Some swear words are common currency and seem to cause little upset while others are so crude and vulgar they raise eyebrows and offend. Generally, festival audiences are quite liberal and profanity like nudity that has a genuine part to play in a short film usually causes few problems.

Always test your dialogue by saying it out loud to see whether it sounds right. Better still, have an actor friend say it. Something that works on the page may not work when you hear it spoken aloud. This is particularly true of long passages of dialogue. Listen to how people around you talk. It can be very revealing and help you write more realistic dialogue.

Don't have characters constantly addressing each other by name. In reality, people seldom use each other's names in conversation. They know who they're talking to! Names are usually only used when the person is the subject of a conversation, when calling to someone – 'Jack! Jack!' – or when directing someone else to them – 'Tell Jack I want him'.

Dialogue is two-way and the writer must take account of the person being spoken to and the context of the conversation. We all change our manner of speech depending on who we're talking to. For example, a police sergeant chatting informally with his constables will suddenly adopt a formal tone when a superior officer appears. People speak differently when faced with formal situations, authority figures or strangers, or when speaking informally with friends, equals and intimates. Using CAPITALS within dialogue indicates SHOUTING. Don't forget to have your characters lie. It's great for plot, conflict and subtext.

Once you complete your screenplay go back through it page-by-page, line-by-line, and ask yourself: can I replace this dialogue with action? Can I find a way to communicate this visually instead of using words? Oscar-nominated director Juanita Wilson said that she often takes all the dialogue out of her finished screenplays then looks to see whether she can still make sense of a scene or the story without it. If she can, she leaves it out; if not she adds back only enough to make it possible to understand what's going on. She has an ability to tell powerful emotional stories using minimal dialogue.

Finally, dialogue is a big subject. Much more could be written about it, but for now remember, in the right circumstances, dialogue can be absolutely spell binding. Film history is littered with classic and memorable dialogue spoken by cleverly crafted movie characters. Do your best to add to the list.

14. CLICHÉS AND STEREOTYPES

Clichés are a curse, the bane of short film. Thousands of short films are produced worldwide every year and many are ruined by clichés and stereotypes. The extent of the problem quickly became apparent to me when I first became a member of a film-festival short-films selection panel and watched scores of films a day. I saw the same things being repeated over and over. Hundreds of films later and I felt like I'd been beaten senseless by every cliché and stereotype in the book, so much so that when I did see something fresh and original it really stood out.

AVOID CLICHÉ

As a writer it's essential to avoid clichés and stereotypes unless you're writing a comedy poking fun at them or deliberately using them to parody or create humour in a scene. You need to be fresh, original and innovative to make your screenplay stand out. Take dramatic risks and give us something that is genuinely new, visually striking, emotionally stimulating or a new take on an old subject. Be ambitious and don't write dull scripts. Stretch the boundaries and avoid ideas that are old and stale.

All clichés were once someone's original idea, ideas that worked so well everybody wanted to copy them. Occasionally, they do still work but that very much depends on the story and situation. They say imitation is the sincerest form of flattery but, unfortunately, in screenwriting, it's a fast track to dull, predictable storytelling.

Clichés irritate audiences because they rehash things – ideas, phrases and characters – that they've seen many times before. The storylines are stale, predictable, use worn-out plot devices and lack originality. Audiences want to be intellectually challenged and emotionally stimulated by something that is bold, new, fresh and original.

STEREOTYPES

Stereotypes are standardised portrayals of people, flawed constructs that assign simplistic fixed characteristics, beliefs, attitudes or attributes to a whole group, class, race or gender of people or to some functional role or occupation. Typically, they're used to label and pigeon-hole people and suggest how they might live their lives. Their spurious assumptions are used to try and predict the behaviour and reactions of people when confronted with problems. It creates caricatures, cardboard cut-outs and flat, lifeless, one-dimensional characters totally lacking in individuality and depth. Such characters are unrepresentative of the real diversity that is human nature.

Two people in the same role, occupation or sharing some other common characteristic or attribute will have very different personalities and will behave very differently in the same situation. Personalities and character traits differ from person to person, that's what makes human beings so interesting. Stereotypes subvert human individuality, personality and psychology.

It is also possible for certain events or situations to become stereotypes. This happens when the actions that occur within the event are described in some standardised way, as a predictable sequence of actions or steps that lead to a predictable conclusion. For example, the stereotypical heist, bank robbery, jailbreak, firing squad, bar-room brawl, gunslingers' duel, hero's last breath and so on. We've seen them many times in movies and they all tend to follow the same recognisable pattern. Break the pattern, turn it on its head and see if you can find a new way to describe it. Create something new. Play against expectations and surprise us.

In short screenplays, clichés and stereotypes typically appear in the following areas:

- Characters and their behaviour

- Dialogue

- Subject matter

- Plot points or devices

CHARACTERS

The clichéd characters found today in short screenplays have often been plundered subconsciously from other stories, films, television shows, novels and plays, unwittingly dragged from memories that lurk half-forgotten in the recesses of the writer's mind.

Some of the most common clichéd characters I've seen include the usual bouncers, hard men and drunks; 'spaced out' hit men for hire and 'zany' Tarantinoesque slackers with guns; prostitutes and stressed-out single mums on benefits; inner-city drug dealers; angst-ridden teenagers; tortured artists; lonely, damaged detectives with drink problems; film-school students making films about film-school students or actors going to auditions; traumatised war veterans; any type of abuse victim; cockney gangsters and arch-villains with cute pets; zombies and werewolves; Hugh Grant doppelgangers; the camp drag queen or tortured gay person struggling to come to terms with his or her secret; the sadistic Nazi and racist Southern sheriff; and, of course, the crazed psycho who won't die. I could go on for hours, there's so many of them. There are sites on the Internet dedicated to movie clichés; check out their lists.

It's not that good stories cannot be written about characters like these. They can be great characters. It's just that they've all been done so many times and portrayed in the same tired old way. The writer needs to find new characters or a new, more original or perhaps realistic way to portray these old, familiar ones. Find an interesting new angle or approach. Study real people and how they behave. Learn a little about human psychology and character traits.

If you're going to write a story about a character inhabiting a certain role, occupation or situation, do what professional actors do: research it, learn about the real people behind the uniform, the façade, the job. Real people in real-life situations often behave very differently from the cliché, often in ways that present the writer with great possibility for creative storytelling and drama. Human motivation, like real life, is complex and very unpredictable. It's a veritable goldmine for the creative writer.

DIALOGUE

Dialogue is also prone to cultural clichés, jargon and slang terms, hackneyed phrases and catchphrases stolen from characters in other films. We all instantly recognise Clint's 'Do you feel lucky, punk?', Arnie's 'I'll be back', Bogart's 'Play it, Sam' and 'Let's go to work' from *Reservoir Dogs*, but if you heard similar phrases coming from the mouths of characters in a short film you'd cringe. When first used, these phrases were original and fitted their character and story; now they've been imitated so often they're more likely to make you laugh. Unfortunately, many stock and clichéd phrases do appear regularly in short films.

Clichéd military and police jargon or gang slang is often taken out of context and used wrongly. Phrases from American cop shows turn up in British police dramas and a variety of short films. Clichéd dialogue often goes hand in hand with clichéd characters. It is as unimaginative as its characters.

Dialogue clichés are particularly common when a screenplay deals with characters from another race, culture or society. Stock phrases appear that are never in fact used in those cultures. We see the same old clichéd wedding-ceremony phrases, police-procedural jargon, courtroom chatter, sexual banter and so on. Characters give predictable, clichéd responses to given situations. Writers need to find more interesting ways to write dialogue. Better still, consider whether the dialogue is even necessary; if not, cut it.

SUBJECT MATTER

The choice of subject and even the location for the story itself can be a cliché. Clichéd story types that have been done to death in short film include anything featuring inner-city misery, depression stories focusing on mental illness, Alzheimer's, dementia, anorexia, bulimia, bipolar disease, suicide, addictions and compulsions, child sex abuse, prostitution, teenage angst, hit men and gangsters, armed robbers, drug deals, homelessness and deprivation, post-traumatic stress, marriage break up and relationship problems, dreams and film-school students navel-gazing, making films about themselves.

Then there are the journeys of personal discovery, mundane 'slice-of-life' stories, the 'nothing happens' stories where people, usually students, crack heads or jive-talking teenagers sit around talking deep and meaningful nonsense – a common bad film-school film – and then there's schoolboy humour. The latter usually involves rubber chickens, inflatable dolls, assorted sex toys and immature 'tee-hee' sex jokes and toilet humour – believe me, avoid it; it just isn't as hilarious as the filmmaker seems to think.

There are so many predictable variations of stories about these subjects that the writer really needs to dig deep to find something new to say. Most are perfectly valid subjects and it appears they're popular because it's felt they can generate intense emotions, which they can. However, the problem is that so many of them are treated in exactly the same way, telling basically the same story. Sometimes, the nature of the subject itself dictates the shape of the story. Once, during a selection day, I watched three short films in quick succession that told an identical Alzheimer's-based story – they had three different directors and came from three different parts of the world. They'd been randomly selected from a pile of discs we had to watch.

Then there are the so-called 'homage' films. These are simply straight rip-offs of some well-known director's work, style or hit film. Copying someone else's work or style represents a poverty of ideas. It doesn't impress festival juries or industry stakeholders. Don't try to copy Tarantino, Hitchcock, Scorsese, or whoever; become the new Tarantino and develop your own style, voice and ideas.

The choice of subject matter also tends to dictate the use of the same clichéd locations – decayed tower blocks, student flats, dingy pubs and smokey shebeens, betting shops and clubs, run-down bedsits and so on. Try to find a new way to approach whatever subject you choose to write about. Find a new story to tell.

PLOT DEVICES

While there is often little room for complicated plotting in a short film, plot clichés do appear, most of which have been pirated from successful feature films and television dramas. Copying twists and surprise endings is particularly attractive because this sort of thing often works well in short film. Think about each beat in the plot of your short film and consider whether it is a cliché. Has it been used before? Can you find a new way to show or express the same thing?

Examples of short-film clichés include alarm-clock and walkabout, *Sex and the City*-style openings, meal preparation, meaningful stares into the camera or a mirror, angst-ridden characters staring moodily out to sea, usually from somewhere high up, or out the window of a moving bus, car or train as it passes scenery, usually with the sun flickering through trees. There are hundreds of clichéd scenes like these, far too many to list.

Then there are the invincible psychopathic killers who always seem to come back to life for one more go at the hero; the war story where the first guy to show his buddies a photo of his girlfriend is guaranteed to die; the courtroom dramas where some new piece of evidence is revealed just in time to save the innocent defendant from certain conviction or death; the sports movie where the hero's team always wins the championship by one point scored at the very last minute. There are countless predictable plot points and clichéd devices to be found in feature films, many of which find their way into short films.

That is not to say they don't have their use. Sometimes they are part of the formula that makes a particular genre of movie work. The Bond franchise is full of them, from the 'James Bond opening' chase sequence and briefing from 'M' to the standard expository showdown between Bond and the arch-villain at the end. Predictable as they are, they're part of Bond lore and audiences love them. It makes the point that, in certain circumstances, cliché can be acceptable. It's just a question of how the writer uses it and what role it plays within the story. Generally, however, cliché doesn't work in short film and is best avoided.

RESEARCH, LIVE LIFE AND WATCH SHORT FILMS

If you intend to write a short screenplay or direct a short film it's essential that you watch as many short films as possible. Check out the competition. Study what everyone else is doing and you'll quickly realise just how common many of these clichés are. Search for new things to write about. Find original stories or new ways to tell old ones and avoid cliché.

I'm concerned that one reason why some short filmmakers slavishly copy cliché from film and television is the limited life experience of the writers and filmmakers themselves. They fail to recognise cliché and stereotyping for what it is or cannot think of a more realistic and believable alternative. A widely varied life experience brings with it a deeper knowledge and broader understanding of life and humanity in general. It gives the writer more material to work with, more ideas, more background information and a greater understanding of how people work and the world around us. It's fertile ground for the creative mind.

One effective way to compensate for limited life experience is research. Thoroughly research whatever it is that you want to write about. There are plenty of sources of information available now in this Internet age. If you plan to write about a local subject go and talk to people who actually know about it, watch what they do, visit the real locations and watch what happens. Find the drama in every story but, most of all, if you want to tell a first-class story and make your screenplay stand out, avoid clichés and stereotypes.

15. LOGLINES, SYNOPSES, OUTLINES AND TREATMENTS

Your first response to this chapter may be to say: I'm only writing a short screenplay so I don't need to learn how to write loglines, synopses, outlines and treatments. They're only for feature-film writers. What relevance do they have to me? In fact, they're very relevant and important skills to master for at least three reasons.

1. A standard requirement for submissions to competitions, funders, production companies and film festivals

2. Useful tools for clarifying, developing and explaining your story

3. Professional screenwriting skills

SUBMISSIONS

If you wish to enter a screenplay competition you will be required to provide a logline and a short summary or synopsis of your script. These typically range from 25 to 50 words for loglines and 100 to 500 words for synopses. All funding organisations and production companies require loglines, synopses and treatments if you apply to them for any kind of support or funding to produce your film. Festival entry forms and Withoutabox, the global online submissions manager, also require them. Short-film press kits also require and include loglines and synopses of differing lengths, typically a quarter page, half page and single page. The producer or director will generally look to the writer to provide them.

STORY DEVELOPMENT

These four techniques – the ability to write loglines, synopses, outlines and treatments – are useful tools to use when developing and clarifying your story before you write it. Each requires a different level of clarity, focus and understanding to be able to reduce the story to its bare essentials. This process helps to diagnose and expose any failings, gaps, contradictions and weaknesses that exist within your story. It helps you to understand how the different parts fit together. Each tool functions at a different level of analysis. Together, they reveal whether your story works. Taking the time to write them will greatly assist your writing process. They also play a useful role in explaining the story to potential producers and directors, when casting actors, recruiting production crew and dealing with anyone else whose assistance is required to produce the film. They answer that most basic of questions, 'What's your story about?'

PROFESSIONAL SKILLS

The ability to write a logline, synopsis, outline and treatment are essential skills that you will need to master if you intend to become a professional screenwriter. It's an essential part of the screenwriter's toolbox and a business requirement. Later in your career you will find they play an important role in selling, marketing and promoting your work. It's another one of those vital transferable skills that you can learn in the training ground that is short film.

LOGLINES

What is a logline? A logline is a simple concise answer to the question, 'What's your story about?' It boils your story down to its bare essentials and encapsulates it in one or two sentences. A compelling logline should convey the fundamentals – who the protagonist is, what he or she wants, and who or what stands in their way. It should promise conflict and drama and create a compelling mental picture of what the story is all about. It should sell the story, stir our curiosity and make us want to know what happens next. The following example is taken from *Gladiator*:

> *When a Roman general is betrayed and his family murdered by a corrupt prince, he returns to Rome as a Gladiator to seek his revenge.*

We can see who the protagonist is – a Roman general – and what stands in his way – a corrupt prince – and his goal: he wants revenge for the murder of his family. We also see the 'how': he returns to Rome as a gladiator. But we aren't told the outcome, so we're curious: how does it all end? This example was taken from a feature film but it's just the same for a short screenplay. This example is from my own short screenplay, *The Day Sam and Ralf Pushed Max Too Far* in Appendix A:

> *Tormented by warring neighbours, a decent old man is forced to intervene to save the life of a child.*

The protagonist is a decent old man, his warring neighbours are the opposing force and his goal is to save the life of a child. There are high stakes and we're promised drama because we know he's going to intervene but we don't know the outcome and hence are left wondering what happens.

Typically, loglines do not reveal the ending, especially when it's a twist. However, there is some debate about this. Loglines used in television or film guides or on the back of a DVD cover would never include the ending as knowing that would spoil the viewer's experience

– knowing the twist ending in *The Sixth Sense*, *The Usual Suspects* or *The Crying Game* would really spoil the enjoyment of watching these films. In these cases the logline is only used to tease the viewer, hook his or her curiosity and generate interest in the film.

However, if a logline is targeted at a funding organisation, a production company or a producer, it might be beneficial to know how powerful the ending is. It might improve the chances that these groups would want to be involved in making the film. A strong ending is much more likely to produce a financially successful film.

A good logline is critically important in hooking interest. It is usually the first thing anyone sees of your script or film and first impressions do count. No matter how clever your logline is, it needs to unwrap your story in an instant. If it doesn't then it hasn't done its job. Take the time to get it right as it will be widely used if your screenplay is produced. It should accurately reflect the story and not oversell or misrepresent it.

Don't confuse a logline with a tagline. A tagline is a one-line phrase used on a movie poster, for example, 'Just when you thought it was safe to go back in the water' from *Jaws 2* or 'In space, no one can hear you scream' from *Alien*. While these are catchy and memorable, they don't actually tell you much about the story.

This is but a brief introduction to loglines but the bottom line is a good logline should succinctly answer the question, 'What's your story about?' It should make you want to read the script or watch the film. This applies equally to both long and short films.

SYNOPSES

A synopsis is a brief summary of the story, written in a simple, easy-to-follow form. It can range in size from as little as 100 words up to as much as 500 words or a page. Any larger and it moves into the territory of outlines and treatments. The synopsis focuses on the main thread and plot of the story. It does not go into complicated detail, subplots, minor characters and so on. At the shorter end the synopsis may amount to little more than an expanded logline.

The longer synopsis deals with the main plot and any significant character changes or arcs that relate to that action. It should mention the character's goals, the stakes, the obstacles and conflict he or she faces, and what action he or she takes to resolve the situation. It should be written in simple prose, in the present tense and in an interesting and lively style. It should flow naturally across several paragraphs and show the script in its best light. It must be an easy read, short but to the point. Could you summarise your 5-, 10- or 15-page short screenplay in, say, 250 or 300 words? You will probably need to write several drafts before you find one you're happy with but it will be worthwhile. Even a 10-page short can contain a surprising amount of activity.

OUTLINES

There are many different interpretations of what an outline is and how long it should be. Many film bodies use the word outline when what they are really looking for is a synopsis. Indeed, sometimes there's little to choose between a long synopsis and a short outline.

Generally, outlines are longer and more detailed and they also tend to be viewed as writers' documents as they help the writer develop the story. Typically, organisations request loglines, synopses and treatments but seldom detailed outlines as well. If you are requested to provide an outline, clarify what it is they want as it can turn out that they're only looking for a synopsis on the one hand or they want a detailed treatment on the other. In some cases an outline may be no more than a more detailed and expanded synopsis but my own preference is for the type of outline commonly known as a step outline or beat sheet. I think it is a much more useful document for a writer to use when preparing to write a script.

In a step outline each scene is reduced to little more than a sentence, one or two lines at most, or a brief paragraph if it's a long scene. This describes in simple terms what happens in that scene. Each step or beat is numbered and listed in the same order that it appears chronologically in the story. It then becomes very easy to read through the entire story and see what works and what doesn't. It can reveal whether there are problems with pace or any unnecessary scenes or story points.

It is also possible to transfer this information to index cards and, if needs be, these can be moved around on a table or wallboard and used to work out a better structure. My step outline for *The Day Sam And Ralf Pushed Max Too Far* was less than three pages long. I have a copy of one for Chinatown that is 10 pages long. I believe step outlines are a useful bridge between synopses and treatments. They help to analyse a story's structure and pace and detect variations in scene length, tempo and plot.

TREATMENTS

A treatment or 'treatment of concept', as it is sometimes known, is a more substantial and detailed document. It's a narrative summation and detailed exploration of a story, its premise and concept, structure, characters, their motivation and goals, the plot, theme, style, conflict, opening and climax. It examines the story in greater depth and tests its viability as a project. The reader wants to 'see' the story and see whether there is enough substance to it to bring it to life on screen.

Treatments are used to sell a script or film and to analyse its story and diagnose any problems within it. It helps to organise the writer's thoughts. Again, while almost mandatory in the feature or television world, the short-screenplay writer also needs to use them for the same two reasons – to organise his or her thoughts before writing the story and then to persuade funding bodies, production companies and producers to invest their time and money in producing the script as a short film. Both these steps are essential if you want to succeed in the long term.

There are a range of opinions as to what makes a good treatment and how they should be written. They are always written in prose, in the present tense and should be active, gripping reads. You should avoid the use of phrases such as 'we see', 'and then', or passive phrases and adverbs. It needs to be entertaining and have some sort of emotional resonance with the reader. It should capture the thrill and emotional impact of the story and make you want to see it. It should be concise and dramatic but should not be an overly detailed or laboured retelling of the story, i.e. this happens... and then this... and then... and then...

There are different models and templates for treatments to be found throughout the screenwriting world but the best one I have found is that taught by literary agent, Julian Friedmann, and set out in his very useful book, *How To Make Money Scriptwriting*. Based on decades of experience Julian devised a four-part template that has proved successful for his many clients. While developed for use with feature film, television and literary projects the same format can also be used by short-screenplay writers. The length of the treatment will just be shorter and more condensed. Julian's template breaks the treatment down into four parts – the introduction, character biographies, statement of intent and storyline.

The introduction is a brief 'hard sell' to pique the curiosity of the reader and is like the blurb on a book jacket or DVD cover. Together with a good title this introduction need only highlight the premise, central character and some key dramatic incident from the story. It hooks the reader's interest but should not oversell, as the storyline will have to live up to this introduction.

The character biographies give the reader a brief insight into who the characters are, especially the main character, their motivation and psychology. In a short screenplay there should only be one main character, the protagonist, an antagonist and a few minor supporting characters. The main character may get a full paragraph, the others only three or four lines each.

The statement of intent says why you want to write this screenplay. It describes your intentions for the piece, your source of inspiration, whether it's based on a true story or personal experience and any other interesting background information. Do you want it to communicate something of importance, a message? It allows the reader to 'place' the story in relation to the writer.

Finally, the narrative storyline. This should be a relatively brief description of the story and its key elements. It should flow and be easy and exciting to read. It should convey the emotion of the piece and capture the drama and essentials of the story.

A lot more can be said about each of these four elements but, for now, the main point to note is that, even though you are only writing a short screenplay, you need to develop these skills. You will find that your screenplay, short film and career will all benefit if you take the time to write each of these short documents.

16. REWRITING

All writing is rewriting. Screenwriters rewrite, it's what we do. You MUST rewrite. You WILL rewrite. I'm being too harsh? Yes and no, but I want to emphasise this point. The number-one reason for rewriting is to improve your screenplay. A better screenplay makes for better storytelling and a better short film. It'll be a better example of your talent and ability and a better calling card. Rewriting is a critical part of the writing process. A good writer is never satisfied and always wants to improve what he has written. Hemingway famously remarked, 'The first draft of everything is garbage,' only he used much more colourful language.

My second reason for saying this is that so many short films fail at birth because of a weak, poorly thought out, boring or unoriginal story and a badly written and underdeveloped screenplay. Find the best story you can, develop it to the full, write the best screenplay possible, then rewrite and refine it until it's the best realisation of that story possible on paper. Do all this BEFORE you shoot your film.

UNDERDEVELOPED SCREENPLAYS

It's a beginner's mistake to stop writing after the first draft and, unfortunately, something that far too many non-writer filmmakers do. With little screenwriting experience they complete the first draft on their own and think that's all they need. As a result the story and film suffer from underdevelopment and problems that become all too apparent during filming and editing. It is possible to make a bad film from a good screenplay for a multitude of reasons – bad acting, poor sound, bad lighting, pedestrian editing – but it's nearly impossible to make a good film from a bad screenplay.

One of my principal reasons for writing this book is the frustration I've felt at seeing so much effort spent by so many filmmakers on producing films that are stillborn because they lack a well-developed story and screenplay. I'm writing this in a week where I've spent three full selection days watching a total of 159 International Short films, and many of them repeated the same mistakes and problems discussed in this book.

It's obvious from the credits that many were written by the director, principal actor or other key participants who clearly lacked screenwriting ability, whatever their other skills. Some do have a fascinating idea at their core but, from what appears on screen, it's clear that the screenplay has been badly written and executed. They include so many basic mistakes that the film never stood a chance. I've watched films with stories that even a mediocre screenwriter could have significantly improved.

If there's a lesson to take from this book it is this: find the best story you can and a skilled writer, then develop that story, write the script, then rewrite, rewrite, rewrite until it's the best thing you can produce. Only then shoot it. Get your blueprint right first. Don't take short cuts. Professional writers know they have to rewrite. They embrace the process. They'll do it for as long as it takes to fine tune the story because they want to produce something they can feel proud of.

THE REWRITING PROCESS

There's rewriting and rewriting. There's the initial ongoing work-in-progress rewriting that takes place everyday as the writer writes the original first draft of the screenplay and revises what he's written the day or even moments before. Then there's the rewriting that is correcting what I call factual errors of typing, spelling, punctuation, grammar and format. Something is spelt right or it is not; correcting it doesn't alter or refine the story. Likewise, correcting grammar or formatting mistakes doesn't change the story. The rewriting I refer to in this chapter is the much more significant rewriting that takes place after the first draft has been completed. It's more substantial and can significantly alter and improve the story and screenplay.

If you take time to plot and outline your story carefully before you begin writing, it will save time in the rewrite. Similarly, cutting unnecessary material during the writing and rewriting process will save time and cost in the shoot and edit.

BACK UP

Before you rewrite, make sure you save the new draft as a separate file. Do the same with each subsequent significant redraft, especially if there are major structural, story or plot changes. Give it a different date or draft number so that if anything goes drastically wrong you will have the earlier draft to fall back on. It goes without saying, I hope, that you, as a professional writer, are automatically backing up all your work to a separate hard drive or storage device or even saving it onto DVD data discs. Don't have the loss of all you've ever written lurking just one hard-drive crash away! Personally, I also like to keep a printed copy of all I write.

TAKE A BREAK

Before attempting to rewrite take a break for a few weeks, deadlines permitting. Put some distance between you and the first draft. It allows your writing brain and creative core time to recharge and subconsciously absorb what you've already written. It's also easier to cut with the passage of time; you're not so attached to what you sweated so hard to create in the first place. Some writers like to revisit their research or even revisit locations and people who inspired them. Now the script's complete you may realise you missed something. Did you capture what it was about those locations and people that inspired you? You might get new ideas for the next draft.

GET FEEDBACK

Constructive feedback will greatly help your rewriting. If possible, show your screenplay to friends whose judgement you trust and who have some knowledge or experience of writing and filmmaking. Ask their opinion. Question them subtly. Be careful not to put words into their mouths. Listen carefully to what they have to say and especially to the reasons they give for their opinion. If several have issues with or comment on the same thing then you may have a problem to fix. Consider the feedback, filter it and pay attention to problem areas.

Family, relatives and non-writing friends are generally unreliable sources of feedback. Their typical response will either be false praise – 'That's great!' – or ridicule – 'Who do you think you are? Steven Spielberg?' Use only those whose opinions and judgement you trust.

Table reads at writers groups or with actors you know can also be invaluable. Sit back and listen to the flow of the story, especially the dialogue and listen to their feedback. Finally, if you have the resources, or are about to shoot it with a substantial budget, it can be useful to pay for some professional feedback and analysis. The advice may save you money in the long run.

READ THE SCREENPLAY

Time has passed. You've gathered feedback and reconsidered your notes. Now you're about to rewrite. Read and reassess the screenplay in full without distractions or interruptions. My personal preference and advice is to do this with a printed copy and pen. Scribble notes as you go. Read it several times over like this, scribbling and marking issues, score out anything you think you can delete and so on. Use these handwritten notes as a guide when you rewrite. Don't worry, you'll think of plenty more as you go.

INTERROGATE YOUR SCRIPT

Some writers prefer to rewrite everything in one go while others prefer to work systematically through their script, focusing on only one thing at a time, e.g. character then dialogue then structure and so on. Whichever approach you adopt you must interrogate your script. Ask questions about each of its elements and seek out problem areas that need to be rewritten. Discovering what doesn't work helps you discover what does. The following sections will suggest some appropriate questions to ask. I'm sure there are many more.

DIALOGUE

Read all dialogue aloud or have someone else do it for you. Does it flow? Is it believable? Is it stilted, clumsy, awkward? Are there any tongue twisters? Is there any rambling dialogue where characters chatter aimlessly about something insignificant? Eliminate it unless there's a specific reason for it. Is the dialogue 'on the nose', repetitive, redundant or 'too talky'? Can you take lines of dialogue out and still convey the meaning you intended? Can you say more with less? Is there enough subtext? Remember: 'show, don't tell.' Review any profanity or crude and vulgar language – do you really need it? Is it true to the character and situation? Can you differentiate the characters by their dialogue or do they all sound like the same person? If it's a comedy, did it work? Did the readers and listeners laugh in the right places?

CHARACTERS

Are my characters believable, strong, memorable and three-dimensional? Are they dull, flat, clichéd or stereotypical? Have I written characters that a professional actor would love to play? Do any of my characters need a make over? Do they look like real people in real trouble? Is the antagonist strong, a worthy opponent? Do my characters have credible motives and goals? Does the protagonist change over the course of the story? Do I care about or emotionally connect with the main character? Are my characters' actions, attitudes and behaviour consistent, believable or plausible? Would a real human being behave like this? Is the character's behaviour contradictory, for example, being terrified of heights yet later jumping a deep chasm? Are there any unnecessary characters? It's important to get the main character right, as we experience the story through them.

STORY, STRUCTURE AND PLOT

Slow, moody openings don't work well in shorts. It's essential to have active openings that hook the audience. Does it open fast? Does the set-up work? Has it got a good hook? Is the problem clear? Is the middle strong enough with enough pace, conflict and complication to hold an audience? Does it sag? Is the ending strong? Does it deliver what it promised in the set-up or is it implausible? Is the resolution satisfying? Does the twist work if it has one? What do you want the audience to think or say as they leave the cinema?

Does the structure need reworking? Is this the best way to tell the story; indeed, is a screenplay even the right form for this story? Is it really a short story or an epic in a matchbox? Does your story know what it is? Is the storytelling clear and consistent or annoyingly predictable?

Challenge every scene, every line of action and dialogue and ask: what's its purpose? Does it serve the story? Is it necessary? If not, cut it. If you have a favourite scene or piece of dialogue but it doesn't serve the story, be ruthless and cut it, save it for another time, another story.

Is the plot plausible? Are there any glaring inconsistencies, holes or flaws? Is there causality? Does A actually cause B? Actions don't happen without a reason. Coincidences make for bad storytelling.

Is the plot weak with too many missing links, contradictions and inconsistencies? Do you hunger to find out what happens next? Is it a page-turner?

Are the stakes big enough? Is there enough conflict? Do the obstacles really challenge the hero? Does the story have rhythm and pace or does it drag in places? Does it have enough spectacle and visual excitement? Don't forget the WOW factor. Is there too much exposition? Have you left enough room for the audience and their desire to try and figure out what's happening as they go along?

Is what originally excited you about the story still there? Ask 'what if' questions to see if you can find an alternative way to present scenes, incidents, plot points, but be careful not to throw the baby out with the bathwater. Can you make the story more dramatic? Is there a moral to your tale? Does the script deliver it? Will the audience get it?

TITLES AND NAMES

Great titles and character names can make a screenplay. Are you still happy with your original title or has the act of writing the script suggested a better one? The majority of great film titles are based on the names of a place or person. However, even bad titles become classics if the film is a huge success. If a screenplay fails to attract attention, the simple act of changing its title can make a difference and get it read.

Are you happy with the names of the characters? Are they evocative and appropriate to the character's personality? Names and nicknames convey a certain image and short names are to be preferred. What image do you have of a Lolita or Samantha? What about Joan and Martha or Bert or Tom? Sometimes you can play with perception for effect; for example, Samantha is a little dowdy old woman and not a sexy siren or Bert is a six-foot City investor and a hunk and not a bricklayer or truck driver. Have you used names that sound too alike and cause confusion?

INTEGRATE CHANGES

Making significant changes to one part of your screenplay can have knock-on effects on something else in your script. Everything you rewrite and change must remain compatible and consistent with the story as a whole. You must integrate all your changes with the whole. It may require changing aspects of the set-up, planting new clues, changing aspects of the character's personality, motivation, goals or behaviour. This is very important if your story and plot are to hold together and remain consistent and plausible.

KNOW WHEN TO STOP

Perfection is an ideal. There comes a point when you've done the best you can and need to stop. What that point is only you can decide. There's no prescription to tell you when. Some screenplays need more work than others but there comes a time to let the bird fly the nest and see whether it soars or plummets. You need to keep everything in perspective. Stop before your rewriting becomes counterproductive and damages the original story. Do your best and be proud of the finished work. No one will know how much rewriting you did; they will see only the finished product. If you're the typical writer you'll probably read it a year from now and see some more changes you want to make. You might even discover that what you've written contains the seeds of a feature.

PRACTICALITIES

Consider the practicalities of shooting what you've written. What difficulties has your script created for the director? Too many characters, special effects, stunts, weapons, difficult locations, weather effects, night scenes, nudity, sex scenes, vehicles, music events, animals and so on can all be costly, difficult to shoot and require a lot of time and money. Does your story really need them?

The producer or director may want you to rewrite and cut some things to make it more practical to shoot. However, there's a downside to this. You don't want to rewrite all that made your screenplay interesting and exciting out of it, leaving it drab and lifeless. Now it's cheap and easy to shoot but dull and boring as well, so why bother? I've watched short films that contained such difficult shots yet the filmmaker still managed to find a way to do it very successfully. It's a difficult balancing act. My advice is to be ambitious with your storytelling but be aware of the resource issues and practicalities as well. Learn what you can about filmmaking. Learn what's possible and what it costs.

Part of the creativity of filmmaking comes from finding imaginative ways to get that look, prop, permission and shot. Some filmmakers thrive on that challenge and produce stand-out films. The bigger the story, the bigger the resources you will need. If you have them then my advice is to go for it, be dramatic, tell a powerful story and impress us. If you don't, find a way to tell an equally powerful story within your limits. Some writers set those limits first and then create a strong story to fit them.

TYPOS AND SPELLINGS

Do not rely on a computer spellchecker when correcting typos and spellings. It will fail to spot mistakes where spellings are correct but the words are used incorrectly such as 'there' and 'their', 'were' and 'wear', 'its' and 'it's', and so on. It will also miss or wrongly flag up spellings that are different in American and UK English such as 'center' and 'centre', 'neighbors' and 'neighbours' or 'realize' and 'realise'. Furthermore, while you should correct typos and spellings all the time, the final systematic proofread should be left until the end as subsequent rewrites could create new errors. Personally, I recommend printing off a hardcopy to proofread, as I find it's easier to miss mistakes on a computer screen than on the page. Proofread it several times or even have a friend with a sharp eye do it for you.

You'd be surprised how many errors can still slip through. Always recheck before submitting it anywhere; you'll still find yet more little errors that escaped the first time!

FINAL CHECKS

- Are character names applied consistently in the dialogue headings?

- Are locations consistently named in the scene headings?

- Are all the parentheticals and personal direction really needed?

- Identify passive verbs and adverbs and eliminate them. Substitute more evocative active verbs.

- Check for and eliminate unnecessary adjectives.

- Is everything written in the present tense?

- Remove dates, draft numbers, copyright warnings and ownership paranoia from the title page or cover.

Now sit back and let your bird fly.

17. SCREENPLAY COMPETITIONS

You've completed your short screenplay but not yet had it produced; what else can you do with it? You could always enter it into one of the many short-screenplay competitions out there. Entering prestigious competitions judged or run by or on behalf of industry insiders and professional film organisations can have a lot of advantages for the writer, but what are they? What are the risks?

TEN REASONS TO ENTER

Why do you want to enter a short-screenplay competition? What's in it for you as a writer? Here are ten good reasons:

1. Production

2. Money prizes

3. Material prizes

4. Script reports and analysis

5. Mentoring, consultancy and counselling

6. Feedback and market testing

7. Exposure and recognition

8. Credits and awards

9. Experience of the submission process

10. Taking the initiative

PRODUCTION

Some reputable competitions such as the British Short Screenplay Competition guarantee to produce the winning script and enter it into key festivals and short-film competitions worldwide. It also premieres the completed short film at BAFTA and gives the writer some high-level industry exposure.

Multi-award winning short film *Ana's Playground* was produced after writer-director Eric Howell's 20-page script won the Los Angeles International Short Screenplay Festival in 2006. It became eligible for Oscar consideration after winning the prize for Best International Short Film at the Foyle Film Festival in November 2009 and was later shortlisted in the final ten for the 2011 Oscars.

MONEY PRIZES

Some competitions offer money prizes. You could use the money to meet personal needs or use it to fund the production of your own short film. However, take note: some competitions state that they offer thousands of dollars in prizes, only for the small print to reveal these are not cash prizes at all. Sometimes, the advertised sum is the total value they place on writing services and other non-monetary items that they include as part of the prize, so read the small print carefully before jumping to the wrong conclusion.

Some competitions offer cash prizes but then stipulate that, as a condition of the competition, it must be used to produce your film using equipment, post-production facilities and even crew hired from the same company that is running the contest. In effect, this reinvests the prize money in the company and generates business for it. On the positive side, you do get your film produced.

MATERIAL PRIZES

These can take many forms: screenwriting software, laptops, subscriptions to screenwriting magazines, free membership of screenwriting or film organisations, tickets to festivals and screenwriting conventions such as Creative Screenwriting's LA Expo, free screenwriting courses, books, vouchers to online shops like Writers Store, free screenplay analysis, screenwriting residentials and so on. All of these can be of great use to the emerging writer while any unwanted material can simply be sold on eBay or passed to colleagues.

SCREENPLAY ANALYSIS

An increasing number of competitions offer script analysis as part of their prize. Some offer basic bullet-point analysis to all entrants or to entrants who meet certain criteria. Indeed, some competitions are directly sponsored and run by script consultancies as a means of attracting business. This is becoming more common in the USA where large competitions employ readers from script agencies. Because it generates a lot of business, some of these agencies are now becoming directly involved as co-sponsors. They typically offer contestants professional script reports at a discounted rate.

Many of these reports are perfectly satisfactory and professionally written and can help you to develop and improve your screenplay, but, as ever, script readers and consultancies vary in quality so make sure you assess the agency and competition first. Well-established, reputable competitions will tend to use reputable agencies and readers with strong industry links. Some major consultancies even offer to waive fees if they find a winning script that they really believe in and wish to promote. As ever, there's a price tag and the best consultants come at a price. You get what you pay for so do your checks. Cheapest might not be best.

MENTORING, CONSULTANCY, COUNSELLING

This can include career guidance from a well-known industry professional such as a 'name' writer or script consultant, guidance through multiple drafts of your next script or assistance pitching your script to production companies and executives.

FEEDBACK AND TESTING

Feedback can be direct, in the form of the screenplay analysis mentioned above, or it can be the indirect, but equally useful, feedback provided by how well it places in each successive round of the competition. Entering competitions that publish each round in full allows you to market test your screenplay. The progress and ranking of your script will give you some idea of the quality of your script relative to the many hundreds of other entries. Advancing through multiple rounds means that multiple readers will have read and approved of your script. Placing highly in, or even winning, several significant competitions increases the chances that industry insiders will take notice of both you and your screenplay.

EXPOSURE AND RECOGNITION

Many competitions, especially in the USA, offer industry exposure as part of their prize package. They state that they have so many production companies, agents, producers or whatever queuing up to see the winner's script. They offer to arrange meetings with agents, development executives and producers and state that they will promote the winner on their website, in various industry publications, in online magazines and electronic mail shots. The level of exposure and its relevance varies and depends on the credibility and significance of the competition and its organisers.

CREDITS AND AWARDS

Winning a prestigious award and placing highly in a high-profile competition – particularly those judged and run by industry professionals – increases your credibility as a writer and provides credits for your writing CV and profile. A writer with a lot of credits to his or her name is much more likely to be taken seriously by the industry. It creates a track record, proves you've more than one script in you, demonstrates that you're serious about pursuing your career and that you've reached a certain level of ability relative to your peers. Of course, producers prefer to see awards for feature scripts as well, but major short-screenplay awards are a significant step along the road, especially for an upcoming writer. Currently, the most influential screenplay competition in the world is the Academy-linked Nicholl Fellowships in California. It receives over 6,000 entries per year.

THE SUBMISSION PROCESS

The submission process gives the writer experience of working to deadlines, making formal submissions and forces him or her – if they're not already doing so – to create intriguing loglines and short synopses for their script. It also forces the writer to look differently at their script, re-evaluating, rewriting and polishing it before sending it out – or, if it fails in one competition, before submitting it to the next competition on their list. It forces you to become organised and professional.

TAKING THE INITIATIVE

By entering competitions your screenplay becomes active. It's no longer lying dormant and unseen in your bottom drawer. Getting it out there could be the first step you take to build the confidence you need to approach producers and production companies with your work. Winning a competition or placing highly will increase your confidence and encourage you to try harder.

SHORT FILMS

That's ten reasons for entering competitions but now some words of warning.

BUYERS BEWARE!

Pick your competitions with care and enter only those with reputable track records and direct industry links. Favour those that publish their results in full round by round. There are many competitions out there and almost anyone can start one but some will do nothing for you or your career. Some are only after your entry fee or business and offer little in return so choose wisely.

CHECK THE SMALL PRINT

Always, always, always, read the small print in the terms and conditions and don't just blindly click the 'I accept' box. In the past, I have come across contests that claimed strange rights to copyright, title and even monies earned from the script if it won their competition and was subsequently produced, so check carefully. Be suspicious if the competition offers little or seems to have no industry names as judges or reputable companies and sponsors attached.

MOVIEBYTES.COM

Moviebytes.com is an American website that lists, rates and provides information on a vast array of script competitions worldwide. It includes regular feedback on competitions, interviews winners and has links to each competition. Its online newsletter provides regular updates and notifications as well as publishing contest results. You can sign up to it for free. *MovieBytes* is a very useful resource that enables writers to identify and assess contests for themselves. Other film-industry and screenwriting websites carry similar links to competitions, some of which are run by their sponsors or by contributors to their sites.

Do your research, check track records and build your own list of favourites.

Check writers' forums and blogs to see what they have to say about specific competitions. You can post your own queries and evaluate the answers. Expect the odd disgruntled reply from somebody who did badly in a particular contest or received a bad script report but weigh it up: is the bulk of the feedback positive or negative? Are the negatives all highlighting the same thing? Do your homework, research, check what others are saying online and then make your choice.

PROMOTION

Some contests in the USA promise to send the winner's script and details to hundreds or even thousands of companies, agencies, producers and development executives. Sometimes this is nothing more than a mass e-mail shot which most recipients will, in all probability, delete. You could do the same thing from your own computer by simply buying a copy of the *Hollywood Creative Directory* and setting up your own publicity shot and mass e-mail list. It's simply carpet-bombing the town with unsolicited e-mails which few will pay attention to. It's the mark of an amateur and 'outsider'.

However, reputable and professional competitions will have long-standing relationships and personal contact with specific companies, agents and industry professionals and will be able to target very specific tailored communications about you and your script to them – contacts that will be taken seriously. They don't need to 'blanket the town'. Again, this emphasises the value of checking the reputation of the competition and its organisers first.

Another variation of the mail-shot approach is to add a short article or notice about you to their regular electronic newsletter, which is then sent out to their usual circulation list of industry people and organisations. It does no harm, of course, just be aware of what they mean when they say they will promote you to a large number of companies, agents and producers.

LOCAL GOALS

You may decide that you only want to enter small festivals or competitions in your own area, not because they offer big prizes but simply because they provide the opportunity to attract local attention and make contacts with local filmmakers who might help to get your film made. No problem. You've tailored your entry to a different goal, one that meets your personal needs at this time.

ENTER EARLY

In general, competitions are attached to film festivals, production companies, broadcasters, film councils and agencies, script consultants, screenwriting or film publications, or manufacturers of filmmaking equipment and resources. Most charge entry fees which rise on a sliding scale as deadlines pass. Enter early when the cost is at its lowest. Furthermore, early entries stand a better chance of receiving a thorough read and assessment. Late entries arrive when the contest is drowning in a tidal wave of last-minute entries. By then the readers are under pressure and unable to spend as much time on each script. Unless your script is brilliant it has less chance of standing out.

If you do win a significant competition, capitalise on it, add it to your writing CV, profile or website. If you're trying to get a local film production company, actor or director interested in helping to produce your film, tell them: 'This is my award-winning script x, which won this award against 500 scripts from 40 countries', or something along those lines. Make use of your credit once you get it. Don't waste it; you earned it.

18. SCREENPLAY CASE STUDY #1

The Day Sam And Ralf Pushed Max Too Far

By

Patrick Nash

In this chapter we will look at the first of our sample screenplays, one of my own called *The Day Sam And Ralf Pushed Max Too Far*. This screenplay was first written in September 2009 and was the Bronze Award winner in the shorts category of Hollywood's PAGE International Screenplay Awards competition in 2010.

Please now read the screenplay in Appendix A and return to this chapter when complete.

Welcome back. What did you think? First impressions? In its original format in Movie Magic Screenwriter 2000 it was exactly 15 pages long, hence I'd expect the finished film to be not much more than 15 minutes in length.

This screenplay is an example of one that deals with a single moment in time. It's also an example of one of my favourite approaches to writing a short script. Begin with what appears to be a normal day then turn it completely upside down. The normality introduces us to the story's world while the abnormality gives us the drama.

Notice how so much is packed into just 15 minutes – life and death stakes, two deaths, a gun and knife, a shooting and stabbing, a violent bully and a teenage Lolita, domestic violence, sexual tension, exhibitionism and voyeurism, love and loss, a heart attack, together with a powerful dilemma and pressure to act. Remember what I said about taking things to the extreme and drama being life with the boring bits cut out.

INSPIRATION

This story was inspired by a series of disturbing television news reports about family meltdown situations in Britain and Ireland where children had been killed. In many of the associated court cases it was revealed that neighbours had long known there was a serious problem next door, had seen and heard things but been too afraid to intervene. I was also struck by the amount of suffering and stress these difficult neighbours had caused, suffering which had sometimes gone on for years without respite.

A secondary source of inspiration was a news discussion about the use of anti-social banning orders – ASBOs – by police and councils trying to control problem families and their children in Britain. Many different types of cases were discussed and these real-life events inspired my story and its original title *Neighbours From Hell*.

THEMES AND ISSUES

What's this story saying? What's the underlying theme or message? We all need good neighbours but we can't choose them or what they do. Good neighbours add value to our lives but bad neighbours destroy it. They ruin our quality of life and damage our health. Do we ignore what's happening next door or do we get involved? Where do we draw the line on what constitutes acceptable behaviour and privacy? Neighbours may be at each other's throats for many reasons – race, religion, sex, national identity, social class, political differences, drink, drugs or even noise – while others are just downright bad. The stress and tension of living with difficult neighbours can be intolerable.

But what if it's more than that? What if lives are at stake? What would you do if you knew that a neighbour's child was at risk because of serious domestic violence and abuse? Would you get involved? Could you live with yourself if a child died because you were too afraid to act? Real people face this dilemma every day.

STORY

I decided to explore these issues by trapping a benign individual between two troublesome neighbours, each of whom posed a different kind of threat. Max would be the harmless old man, a pensioner and an army veteran, someone who'd recently lost his wife and had a heart condition. He just wants to live out his remaining years in peace but I decided to put him under extreme pressure using those two great staples of movie plots, sex and violence. On one side there'd be Ralf Baxter and his brutal reign of domestic terror while on the other there'd be teenage Lolita, Sam Taylor, and her sexual provocation.

Initially Sam's character was to play a larger, more aggressive role in the story but I decided that it would be impossible to keep two separate stories going at the same time within the timeframe available. I had to choose one so I decided to place all the emphasis on the Baxters' domestic-violence storyline while keeping the hint of sexual tension present, with Sam taunting and teasing Max while sunbathing topless. You simply can't overdo it in a short. One main plot or storyline is enough.

I then considered what the stakes would be? What could I do that would take it to the extreme? What would push Max over the edge? It was obvious from the real-life court cases that the most powerful dilemma faced in such situations was a life-or-death one involving the life of a child. I decided that Ralf would threaten the life of one of his kids and, to make the threat more credible, immediate and dramatic for Max, he'd wound Janice first. What would Max do? He's forced to decide within seconds whether to intervene and save the child's life or sit back and pretend not to know what's going on. What will be the consequences for Max and the Baxters if he decides to act, or, then again, if he decides not to?

Many of the people in real-life neighbours-from-hell situations complain of the effect the stress has on their health. This gave me the idea for Max's heart condition and I decided to use it as the subplot. It would be the ticking time bomb in the story. Every incident and escalation would pump up the pressure on Max's heart until finally it was too much to bear. The shooting would be the final straw.

Putting pressure on Max's heart was one of the reasons for keeping Sam's involvement in the story. I debated for a time whether Max's voyeuristic behaviour needed to be qualified or softened. I considered having Max turn away to look at a photo in his bedroom showing his wife in younger days bearing a striking resemblance to Sam in the face. Hence, it would appear as if she reminded him of his wife and the sexual part of his life that no longer existed. In the end I decided not to explain. Let people wonder.

STRUCTURE

This short follows the traditional beginning, middle and end structure with a set-up, conflict and resolution. There is escalating conflict and tension with a surprise or unexpected ending – when you see Max collect his newspaper and milk at the start, do you expect him to shoot someone dead half an hour later and die of a heart attack on his kitchen floor?

The beginning covers the first few pages, from Max's first appearance on his doorstep to the introduction of the Baxters and their domestic row. It establishes the location and introduces Max as a lonely old man with a heart condition who is upset by his neighbour's violence. It also introduces the Baxters, Ralf's violent temperament and their volatile family life. We witness his latest violence against Janice and the children. The turning point comes when the Baxters' row escalates and moves into the back garden.

The middle part shows the escalating conflict between the Baxters, resulting in Janice being stabbed. It also adds the sexual dimension of Sam, the exhibitionist next door, and the effect of her behaviour on Max. The middle reveals Max's increasing concern for the safety of Janice and the kids and the impact of this and Sam's antics on his blood pressure and heart condition. The point of no return for Max comes when Ralf holds the knife to Liam's throat. What is he to do? He decides to act and searches for his old army souvenir, a revolver. This fateful decision takes us to the climax of the story.

Max confronts Ralf at gunpoint, but when Ralf refuses to back down a sudden movement of the knife causes the stressed-out Max to fire. Suddenly, everything changes: shock, horror, Ralf is dead. His family unexpectedly flock to his body crying with grief. Max tries to justify firing to the onlookers but the pressure on his heart finally gives way. He staggers away to die on his kitchen floor clutching the picture of his beloved wife.

Max's decision to intervene brings death to both him and Ralf, but what would the consequences have been for Janice and the kids if he hadn't acted we can only guess. In the closing sequence we see Sam as she truly is – a child frightened out of her teenage sex fantasy into reality. She shrinks away from Max, shyly trying to cover her breasts where moments before she'd been only too happy to tease him with them, albeit at a safe distance.

In the structure, note the circular dimension to the story. It begins with Max in his kitchen with his heart pills and wife's picture and ends with him back in the kitchen, desperately trying to reach his pills and clutching his wife's picture as he dies. The story has come full circle.

Additionally, note how the first page sets up the story. Max's pills and heart condition, the old army-buddies photo to help explain the revolver, the sound of the row next door, Max's use of a glass to eavesdrop, his wife's photo – everything is there for a reason. Max's heart condition is the subplot, the ticking time bomb that will ultimately take his life.

DIALOGUE

It is worth noting how sparse Max and Sam's dialogue is for principal characters. Max barely speaks until page 11 of the screenplay and says only 80 words the entire script. Sam speaks only five times, saying 10 words. It is Ralf and Janice who do most of the talking – not surprising, as they're having a bitter row. It highlights the point that it's not always necessary to have characters speak a lot; they can do so much with just the visuals. With hindsight I can see bits of dialogue and exposition that I'd like to trim and remove but I decided to leave the script in its original form. For a writer, a script is always a work in progress. There's always something to modify, tighten or add. That is the nature of the process of being a writer.

TITLE

The initial title was 'Neighbours From Hell' but I later decided to change it to 'The Day Sam And Ralf Pushed Max Too Far'. I felt the second title was more interesting as it implied both conflict and some kind of violent showdown or dramatic confrontation. It also named the three principal characters and concealed the fact that Sam was actually a girl. Choosing a good title can be as important for a short as choosing good names for your characters.

LOGLINE

When you enter a competition or apply for funding you will need a logline for your screenplay as well as a short synopsis. The following are three of the loglines I've used with this short screenplay. Each has a certain something and represents a progression in my attempts to find the best one.

- Pensioner Max Montgomery is a reasonable man who just wants to live out his final days in peace. But when wildcat neighbours, Sam and Ralf, assail him from all sides with a barrage of sex and violence, something's got to give – one sunny morning in June it does.

- A decent old man is caught in a terrible dilemma, trapped between the neighbours from hell. When a child's life is at stake, he does the only thing he can and pays for it with his life.

- Tormented by warring neighbours, a decent old man is forced to intervene to save the life of a child.

PRODUCTION

Finally, what kind of issues would this script pose for production? Could it be shot? Yes, but it would not be one for a beginner and it would need a reasonable budget. Of the 24 scenes in the short, four main scenes make up 60 per cent of the script. Many of the short scenes between Max and Sam could simply be shot as long takes and intercut in the edit suite.

On analysis, 60 per cent of the script is set outdoors so a sunny day is required. Bad weather might pose a problem. It will be necessary to be flexible and have a contingency plan and to shoot the indoor scenes if it rains. The use of a realistic-looking gun out of doors will require a special licence, police permission and the hire of an armourer, as will the special-effect shot. The blood splash on the wall behind Ralf might prove troublesome to clean and reset if more than one take is required. Janice and Ralf's scuffle with the knife will require a lot of care to avoid real injury, while using child actors will require special child-actor permits and a chaperone for each.

Sam's topless-sunbathing scene could cause problems. First, finding a suitable and willing actor. She'd have to be someone older who could play younger. Screening would be required to shoot these scenes on location without half the neighbourhood turning up to watch. Finding a suitable street location like the one described in the screenplay should not be a major problem as that street layout was commonly used in post-war housing builds in Britain. However, it might be more difficult to find one where the occupants or owners are willing to allow their property to be used. Two house interiors and three adjoining back gardens in the same street would be required.

Finally, there's the number of actors to be cast – five adults: Max, Ralf, Janice, Sam and her mother; three children: Liam, Alice and the little girl who sticks her tongue out; and a number of extras as neighbours, three of whom speak. This will increase the cost of the production and take time.

Now to our next screenplay, the Oscar-nominated film *The Door*.

19. SCREENPLAY CASE STUDY #2

The Door

By

Juanita Wilson

In this chapter we look at our second case study, Juanita Wilson's screenplay for her Oscar-nominated short film *The Door*. This screenplay is unusual for short-film screenplays in that it is both an adaptation and a true story.

The screenplay was based on the three-page testimony of a Chernobyl survivor, Nikolai Fomich Kalugin, contained in the book *Voices From Chernobyl: The Oral History of a Nuclear Disaster*, compiled by Ukrainian journalist, Svetlana Alexievich. Nikolai's testimony is called *Monologue about a Whole Life Written Down on Doors*.

The Door qualified for Oscar consideration by winning the award for Best Irish Short Film at the Foyle Film Festival in 2008. In 2009 it was nominated for the Academy Award for Best Live Action Short Film at the 82nd Academy Awards. It has also won awards at festivals in Cork, Bilbao, Sarajevo and Warsaw and, in 2008, won the Irish Film & Television Award for Best Irish Short Film. Further information can be found on its official website at www.thedoorshortfilm.com and the film can – at the time of writing – be viewed on Vimeo.

In 1997, Juanita and her partner, James Flynn, founded Metropolitan Films in Dublin and then, in 2002, Juanita, James and Morgan O'Sullivan founded Octagon Films based at Ardmore Studios in Ireland. Juanita has been a producer as well as writer and director. Octagon Films has produced many projects for film and television, most recently *The Tudors*, Neil Jordan's *Ondine, The Borgias* and Juanita's first feature, *As If I Am Not There*. Further information can be found at www.octagonfilms.com.

In January 2011 *Variety Magazine* in Hollywood named Juanita one of its ten directors to watch in 2011.

Please now read Juanita's original screenplay in Appendix B and return to this chapter when complete.

The following interview took place in July 2011 when Juanita attended a screening of her first feature film as director, the award-winning and deeply moving Bosnian war drama, *As If I Am Not There*, at the Queens Film Theatre in Belfast. The interview focuses on Juanita's experience writing and directing *The Door*.

INTERVIEW WITH JUANITA WILSON

How did you learn to write screenplays?

I didn't have any formal training as such but Screen Training Ireland ran some really good training courses and workshops, and they were absolutely fantastic. I learnt a lot from that but it was very daunting too. That was when I was writing the feature, but in terms of *The Door*... *The Door* kind of wrote itself based on the testimony.

How did the testimony help you?

It's a very short testimony, a few pages, and once I worked out a structure for it, starting at the end then revealing what happens, it came together as a series of vignettes or memories. It's as if the man, Nikolai, is trying to recollect what happened to him and make sense of it. They're like separate moments that he's just remembered, key moments of what happened.

Instinctively, I guessed that a lot of the drama should happen offscreen, for example, the scene with the doctor where he's obviously going to tell them that their daughter is very sick, it seemed better that he didn't say anything. I learnt through trying to write that scene that really you can say everything you need if you just set the circumstances up right and then let the audience join the dots. I was lucky with the actors because their faces said so much, more than any words could. This project was quite unique in terms of how it came together.

You had a background in producing, what made you want to write and direct a short?

I actually started off in fine art, in sculpture, and I've always been interested in the idea behind something and in communicating that idea. I was always interested in the creative end of things and I've always written bits and pieces, scraps of things. When it came to film, myself and James Flynn, my partner, set up a company to make films but we weren't really concerned whether we were producers or what. It wasn't that I wanted to be a producer; I just started off that way. It was a fascinating way to learn about the industry because you see every aspect of filmmaking. It was a very valuable experience. I was honoured to produce *H3* and *Inside I'm Dancing* but, as a producer, I found that it was hard to get the creative fulfilment I wanted so I just felt it was time to try and do it myself and be more involved.

Had you any other short-film ideas that you were considering before *The Door*?

Yes, I'd written something very different which was fictional but I'd been reading short stories all the time, looking for something, always trying to work out what would be a good one to do. It was only when I found *The Door* that I really felt, okay, this deserves to be made. It was strong enough for me to ask other people to be involved. I felt the subject was important and that gave me great strength. It brought the right team behind me.

How did you find *Voices from Chernobyl*?

I was reading the *Guardian* book reviews and it was reviewing the book. There was one little excerpt about Nikolai stealing the door and driving it on the back of his motorbike through the forest at night, and, as an image, I thought, 'Wow! That's amazing and it's a true story.' I thought it was very Gogolesque, so I immediately rang them up and ordered the book. As I read it, I just thought, 'Wow!' We bought the rights to that story. It just stayed in my mind and once that happens it just takes on a life of its own.

Had you any problem getting the rights?

No, Svetlana [Alexeivich] had the rights to the book but we haven't been able to get hold of Nikolai. We tried in both Kiev and Belarus but he seems to have just disappeared. I really hope some day we'll find him.

How did you go about adapting it?

The main thing was the structure because if you reveal what it's all about at the beginning then it loses its point, so the idea was to keep the reveal until the end. I love the idea of playing with the audience a little bit, you know, set it up so that they don't know whether this person is a burglar, insane or what, then let them see just enough to wonder what's going on. They have to work it out, then they realise, oh, something terrible happened to this man. It makes it a much more active experience for the audience. I think in a way that's what gives it emotion; it comes at you sideways. A lot of people say to me,

'I didn't realise it was about Chernobyl until the end.' I think that's great because at the end of the day it's really about loss.

Was that the theme? Loss?

Yes, and also about reclaiming human dignity, which is all you can do when you've lost everything else. I think the idea of a ritual is reclaiming something so that, even if you lose the most precious thing in life, you determine the manner in which it will be dealt with, and, for Nikolai, that was within his own family tradition with the door. It gave him a sense of peace that he'd buried his daughter in the manner that was correct for him.

How did you come up with what I call the 'running man' opening?

That came about when we saw Pripyat in the snow on the Internet. We knew we just had to go there. We waited about six months to get permission then went to have a look and it's just the way the city is, it speaks so much, long streets, big buildings, the dereliction, the Ferris wheel and abandoned fairground, the child and lost childhood, everything about that was perfect. We walked and walked around the city and very quickly said we'll use this shot, this angle, whatever. You see man being a victim of his environment, this huge structure and this little man lost within it looking for somewhere. The idea just works. We were lucky to go to Pripyat; without that we would've had to use the apartment. It wouldn't have had the same impact.

How many drafts did it take?

Really only one or two, with some tweaks; nothing changed significantly. In the last version I added in the evacuation scene or made it a little bit bigger. We did get feedback from an editor friend of ours, and a couple of other people, but it just felt right. With your first project, I guess it's important to follow what feels right to you emotionally and visually.

Did your experience as a producer help you when you were writing?

One thing, when you see a script being shot and then see what gets edited and what gets used, it helps you understand what's not needed. I think if you get to the point where you can see in advance – I won't need this, I won't need that – then that's when you really understand the craft.

One of the things that struck me about *The Door* and *As If I Am Not There* is how you have a knack of being able to say so much using just images and pictures with absolutely minimal dialogue. In *The Door*, for example, there are only 25 lines of dialogue in some 17 minutes of film. The main character, Nikolai, barely says 100 words yet it's so powerful, the emotions it conveys.

Yes, I think both subjects are quite strong and sad, people in desperate situations, so you probably don't need to talk your way through them in that sense. It'd be different if they were sitting in a café or something. I do think we rely way too much on exposition and it makes you very impatient, you know, when someone tells you something, then shows you, it gets very annoying. Exposition is to be avoided wherever possible. Assume the audience will know and work out what they need to work out because, by and large, they can.

I think it's always interesting as an exercise to take out the dialogue in your scenes, just take it all out then see what bits you really need. If you've written all the reactions and thought processes well, then you'll find you probably don't need half the dialogue. You'll find the story will tell itself. Just put back in the bits you really do still need. Dialogue takes much longer to hear than you ever think. When you write it you think it's okay but if you're actually waiting with a camera for someone to speak you find yourself asking, do I really need so many words. It's important to learn economy of words.

Had you any other titles in mind other than *The Door*?

Probably, but I just liked *The Door* because it's so symbolic and strong and it doesn't give away anything emotionally or story wise. It's a bit deadpan but it just seemed to the point. It's about the door but obviously, at the end, it's not.

Were there any unforeseen difficulties or anything that with hindsight you'd like to have added in or changed?

No, I don't think so. Sometimes I wonder should I have done this or that, but it's in terms of staging, camera movement and that kind of thing, not in terms of the beats of the story. You could fiddle away forever but then you wonder would you change the emotional dynamic if you did this or that.

Because it's a deeply personal true story were you ever tempted to fictionalise it to make it easier to shoot somewhere else?

No, not really, not with this one, but I could understand that you might need to in some situations, especially with some victim stories where people are still struggling emotionally to come to terms with things. You might need to dramatise it to make things more active.

How did you deal with the ethics of telling such an emotionally challenging true story, respecting what people went through?

It's a great honour to be entrusted with that kind of material and a great responsibility as well. You're kind of blessed and cursed if you have good source material because you really want to deliver something that is of the same standard and impact as the book, but you also have to think long and hard. Are you doing justice to this person? Are you portraying them correctly, their situation and reactions?

I love the idea that I'm like a torch shining a light on something I believe is important and, through illuminating it, other people can see it and make up their own minds. You're part of a process that starts with the real person and then, through someone like Svetlana or Slavenka – author of *As If I Am Not There* – they manage to bring it all together, and then I do my little thing and an audience can see it.

It's nice to be a part of a process of communication like that but it is something you really wrestle with. You have the pressures of dramatic storytelling and you have to respect your audience as well. You can't just document the truth; you also have to present something that works in the format you're choosing to tell the story in. It's something you grapple with all the time.

The usual rule of thumb is a page a minute but you managed to make a 17-minute film from a five-page script. That's quite unusual.

I know, the producers were a bit worried. I think it's the fact that one line can suggest so much. When we went there, the land and the people were so visually and emotionally beautiful, and with all they've been through, there's something very poetic, very romantic and very tragic about it.

Did you always want to direct or was there a point when you said, you know, I'd prefer to let some else do this?

I guess it always feels like the safer option to hand it over to somebody else, but, at the same time, I just felt so personally involved with it and my whole motivation was to make something myself. The hard thing is you're actually trying to convince people that you're going to do something that you don't know you can do yourself, and that is terrifying. You've nothing to fall back on but it's a great adventure. When I found the team that I was lucky enough to find a lot of those doubts were dispelled and their belief, skills and experience carried me through.

What advice would you give to any writer who's thinking of directing?

First of all to make absolutely sure that they really, really love their material and that they know it really well, so that any actor, any member of the creative team, can ask them any question and they can answer and give a reason why this happens or that happens. It's your only job. Everything else someone will help you with, but if you don't know your material you're not in a position to try and direct it. It's your responsibility.

The other thing, I think it's critical to get the right team, to get people who see the project the way you do, that you complement one another and have the right approach, because if there's a mismatch it'll make it difficult for everybody and the work will suffer. Find likeminded people who you trust and who boost each other's confidence.

What about a director who's thinking of writing his own material?

If you're strong visually or story wise then it should be reflected in the script but I think it's really important to learn as much as you can. Get advice, training, help, whatever, even read Syd Field. It was the first thing I did years ago and while it's very formulaic in some ways, it has the basis of everything in it. It's good to learn as much as you can, you can reject or turn it on its head later but it's important to learn a bit about it first.

For me, in terms of scripts, structure is the most important thing; it's the backbone of everything. I think if you get the structure right you can forgive having too much dialogue, too little dialogue, too much whatever, but if the structure's all over the place, no matter how great the scenes or dialogue, if the pace is all over the place and there's no clarity, the audience will get impatient. I would say to anybody who's writing, structure is the thing.

How do you look for ideas? What attracts you to certain things?

I trawl really widely. I spend a lot of time in bookshops – I guess that's one of my primary sources – or scouring the papers for interesting ideas or stories. I suppose what I'm always looking for is a kind of human dilemma, you know where you would say, what would I do in that situation, or imagine if you were here and all this happened, how would I survive, what would I do? Something that has an emotional impact for me, something I connect to. Does this feel real? Is it something I can relate to? Is it strong enough?

Have you ever written anything in another format?

I wrote a novella, for my own amusement, and also some short stories. Short story is an amazing format. I love it. I think it requires rigour and craft to be able to write something like that and not overwrite it. Short films are exactly the same but I think a short film should work more like a poem, present an idea and leave you thinking about it. I think a really powerful short film should provoke thought rather than just tell you a story so that when you leave the cinema you have questions in your head. If you can do that you've done your job well.

With the Oscar nomination, *Variety* in Hollywood naming you one of its ten directors to watch in 2011 and the impact of your first feature, *As If I Am Not There*, what are your plans for the future?

It's really heartening to get that recognition but, at the end of the day, you're only really ever as good as your next script. If they – people in LA – like your script they'll talk to you, if they don't they won't. But it's always helpful to get the recognition. At the moment I'm adapting a book by an American author, Daniel Woodrell, called *The Ones You Do*. It's deliberately completely different from what I've done before. I've also just bought the rights to four short stories by a young Peruvian writer, set in Lima, about people struggling on a day-to-day basis with quite big decisions. My plan is to weave them together somehow but I don't know if it'll work yet.

20. SCREENPLAY CASE STUDY #3

The Crush

By

Michael Creagh

This chapter looks at Michael Creagh's Oscar-nominated film, *The Crush*. Shot in Ireland over three days at Easter 2009 this 15-minute short film was nominated for the live-action short-film Oscar at the 83rd Academy Awards in 2011 after winning the award for Best Irish Short Film at the 2009 Foyle Film Festival. It also received a Special Jury Mention at Robert De Niro's Tribeca Film Festival in New York in 2010, in effect second place. *The Crush* was Michael's first short screenplay and first film as a director.

Please now read the screenplay in Appendix C and return to this chapter when complete.

The following interview took place in Belfast, in August 2011, during a visit by Michael to his hometown. After studying at the Art College in York Street, Belfast, Michael moved to Dublin where he worked for over 15 years as an Art Director in commercial advertising. Recently turned freelance, he's directed several commercials while continuing to write. He currently has a feature-length screenplay set in the Belfast Blitz of 1941 with the Irish Film Board and is working on another set during the Irish Famine.

INTERVIEW WITH MICHAEL CREAGH

Was *The Crush* your first screenplay?

No, the first thing I tried was an idea I'd had in college, a Troubles story, but the thought of writing something 90 to 120 pages long was daunting. I'm used to writing 60-second commercials. But after a while I thought, okay, maybe I can do this, so I wrote it. It was first called '*The Cell*' and later '*The ASU*', about a middle-class Belfast boy living in a nice area who gets caught up with the IRA. I thought of it like a Belfast *Goodfellas*. It was the first thing I wrote. That was 15 years ago. I'd probably cringe if I read bits of it now.

For a long time I also wanted to write something about the Famine. I've churned it over in my head for years. You always know when you're going to write something because it sticks with you. You might have 30 ideas in your head but there's always a couple that keep knocking at the door. I call them 'sticky ideas'. The ones that keep growing, keep coming back, you know there must be a reason. You know when a story excites you. I keep loads of little moleskin notebooks lying around half full of ideas and scribblings.

How did *The Crush* come about?

I always think it was the train journey coming home from the agency in Dublin to where I lived in the Skerries. On my daily commute I'd always be turning things over in my head. I always wanted to do a short, in fact every creative person I knew in advertising talked about it, you know: 'Some day I'm going to write a short, make a short and get into film.' We were all like that but I was determined it was going to happen and not just to write it but to direct it as well. I thought, I've learned enough about writing, I've plenty of contacts and my brother Jim's a BBC cameraman. I just thought: I can do this. A lot of my procrastination was waiting for a story.

So what was the inspiration?

I'd two or three ideas floating but I just felt they weren't exciting enough. I kept waiting for something else. Sometimes you work with kids in advertising and you see them perform and they're just so natural. There's an aaaaah factor. People like kids being at the centre of a story. I always loved Stephen Daldry's *Eight* so I started to think about a story with a kid and I thought, what about a kid with a crush on his teacher? It seemed like a fairly standard, simple, little story. I thought there might be something in the idea but I parked it for a while. Then, later, on that train journey home, I was wondering – how can I make this more interesting? How can I put some drama and twists into it, something that'd really make people watch? Then I hit on the notion of love rivals. We all know kids have crushes and there can be love rivals over a woman so what if we bring the two ideas together, that would be more interesting.

Did the idea of his dad as a cop with a gun come at the same time?

I think the idea of a kid challenging a grown man to a duel came first. I thought a scene like that would be funny. It would have an inherent humour especially if you play it flat and the kid has total conviction. Then I thought, what if I throw in a real gun or what looks like a real gun for some real jeopardy. If there's a real possibility of death then that takes everything up a notch. But I worried about the plausibility of introducing the gun, you know, where would he get it? I also worried about going from one tone to another.

I think the appearance of the gun did take the story to another level because you know then that something more serious is going

to happen. It's that old Hitchcock thing, if you show the audience a gun in Act 1, it'd better fire by Act 3.

Yes, but it took a while to get the subplot right, to set it up and make it seem plausible. I think sometimes surprises don't work because people just go... 'What? Where'd that come from?' You need to drop little clues first so audiences aren't surprised. It's not always about shock. Weaving it in from the start helped build the subplot and increase its plausibility. That was important. Once I got that thread I was able to pull it all together. In advertising you don't show or say anything that isn't relevant and in film it's the same. If you see or hear anything it has to have some relevance to the story. A short film has too little time to be waffling.

How long did it actually take to write?

Not that long. I was thinking about it a lot on the train and making little notes. I worked out the general storyline quite quickly once I'd the hook that he's got a crush on his teacher. I'd the basic story in one of my moleskins. I left it for a few weeks then went back to it and worked out a plan. I decided it was going to be 15 pages and I'd approach it like a feature with a structure, three acts and turning points. Some people criticised me for doing that, treating it like a mini film, but it worked. It focused my mind. Because I was only allowing myself 15 minutes I had to do in the first minute or two what a feature would do in 10 minutes or more, establish a set-up. In fact, we established that the kid was in love with his teacher in the first 30 seconds or so. It was all visuals. That allowed us more time to get into the story but sometimes I worried that I was trying to do too much plot in a short space of time.

Why did you set yourself a 15-minute limit?

I'd read a lot about how to write features so when I decided to do a short I bought books on how to write a short as well. Everything I read seemed to say that 15 minutes is ample – 10 minutes is great, 15 minutes is fine, but if you go over 15 you need to be really good, so maybe it was a lack of confidence, but I decided I'd more chance of losing people if I went over 15 minutes.

How did you learn to write screenplays?

After writing my first feature script and thinking about the Famine story I put myself through screenplay-writing school. I didn't do any courses as such but I bought loads of books. I decided I was going to learn how to write a screenplay properly. I learned about formatting, the three-act structure and all the things you need to know. In advertising it's very free form; different writers could each have very different-looking scripts. But everything I read about film seemed to say that there was a lot of discipline involved. Serious producers wanted everything done in a certain way. It had to be formatted correctly with 12 point courier, double spacing and so on because, if it's not, it goes in the bin. They just think you're not serious. It sounds ridiculous but if you want to get through you have to play the game. It's all there for a reason. A page a minute is handy too.

What screenplay formatter do you use?

Final Draft but up to three years ago I was using Word, setting all the tabs and stuff. *The Crush* was written on Final Draft. I actually love it because when I was younger I was quite a flowery writer but script is so minimalist. It's the perfect format for getting rid of all your superfluous prose. You can't say a lot of things in a script because you can't shoot them; it's as simple as that. You can't shoot 'he was feeling such and such' and so on. You're writing a working document for actors and others to look at so it needs to be right.

Do you think working in commercials helped you?

It's a visual medium like film. Being less wordy is an advantage. You learn economy in commercials because you're not only dealing with a time constriction, you're dealing with people's money and, even though you're writing in words, you're still writing with the pictures in your head. It is different, though. You can't just hop from one to the other. You do have to learn how to do things a different way. I think advertising at its best is also about storytelling.

Did you consider any other titles?

In advertising we'd usually settle very quickly on single-word titles for our projects, like working titles; one word, basic, that's it. I'm not very arty about my titles. If I can sum it up in one word I'll do it. *The Crush* was about a crush, that's it, quick, straightforward, descriptive.

Did anything cause you particular difficulty during writing?

I worried that I was trying to put too much plot in. I was afraid it would be a mess when it got to screen. If you're lucky enough to have people who know what they're talking about get them to read it. I got people like Lenny Abrahamson and other directors I'd worked with on commercials to read it. A couple of little things needed some work but once I spoke to people who knew what they were talking about and they thought it was okay, I wasn't worried.

Did you have a particular theme in mind for *The Crush*?

Well, I see myself as a bit of a cynical romantic. I wanted realism but I like a bit of darkness too. A lot of people have said to me about *The Crush*, should he not have actually shot the guy, maybe it would've said more. Well no, that wasn't the story I was writing. I was writing a love story about a schoolboy but one that has a dark side to it. I wasn't writing a tragedy.

Some of the Americans at the awards asked me, was it about gun crime and kids with guns? It wasn't about anything like that at all. In fact, I deliberately didn't set it in the North – of Ireland – or in Belfast with northern actors and accents because it would've given the wrong impression. People would've thought it was something to do with the Troubles. No, it had Dublin accents and it's a love story with a little dark twist.

It was important for me that he gets the girl in the end. That scene where he and the teacher walk off into the sunset was meant to be like a western. He's won the duel and he gets the girl. I wanted it to be entertaining. It always surprises me that people don't make shorts more entertaining because, if you've less likelihood of being watched, should you not be trying harder to entertain the audience and grab them? So many shorts just aren't entertaining.

Have you any advice for writers wanting to write a short screenplay?

Tell a story and always keep the audience in mind. It's not so much about the subject matter as telling a good story. It has to be something the audience want to watch. If you want to experiment or practise your art, fine, but too many are spending thousands on 'the art of nothingness' films. This writing stories about nothingness is, I don't know... [*Michael makes a gesture of despair*] My motto is: don't be boring. You're working in a medium that the general public doesn't really want to watch so try harder, don't be boring. Win the audience. Don't treat them as imbeciles, respect them, engage with them and don't be boring.

I always worry when I hear people saying 'write what you know' because it's so full of misunderstanding. It's a dangerous cliché. Students and amateurs are always being told it by some tutor or drama teacher. That's all very well but you know George Lucas never actually went into space but he did know about love, about relationships. He did know emotional things like that so he was writing what he knew but doing it with spaceships. Spielberg never actually found an alien in his back garden but he did know about friendship and the hurt of his parents divorcing and the pain of a friend leaving so he was writing what he knew but with aliens. But so many think 'write what you know' means just take a section of your life and write about it, that's not right.

I think you also need to remember you're not writing reality no matter how realistic the effect is that you're going for. You're writing a version of reality, a heightened reality. You're writing drama. What matters is not that something is real but that it feels authentic. Authenticity is very important. Richard Donner said his key word for everything he did when making *Superman* was verisimilitude, which means something like the appearance or semblance of truth or reality. It's like people should believe that this is happening or can happen. His tagline was 'you'll believe that a man can fly' and us kids did. You can lose your audience so easily if they don't believe in the authenticity of what you're showing them. One dumb thing and you're gone. It's all about authenticity.

Have you any advice for writers wanting to direct?

Take an acting course. I did one before I did *The Crush* to learn how actors work. It helped so much. I love actors and what they do. I love seeing how they work and what they can do with words. Always respect your actors and make your writing as good as it can be for them.

Secondly, I self-funded my film and it's a nightmare. I wouldn't advise anybody to do that. I wasn't eligible for some of the schemes but I was so determined to get it made I decided I'd self-fund it with some of my own savings, money from my dad and a bank loan which I'm still paying off. I don't advise anybody to do it that way. I just wanted to shoot it that Easter and couldn't wait any longer. I was so determined to get it made with whatever resources and contacts I had. It's scary but it's a lot of fun as well. I loved it and I can't wait to get behind the camera again.

APPENDICES

APPENDIX A

Short Screenplay:

The Day Sam and Ralf Pushed Max Too Far

By

Patrick Nash

2010 Page Awards Bronze Award Winner

Note: As far as possible original formatting has been preserved with only minor adjustments to meet the needs of publication in book format. The original page numbers have been dropped as, in this published format, the page length is different. The original version, which was formatted in Movie Magic Screenwriter 2000, was exactly 15 pages long. This screenplay should be read in conjunction with the chapter entitled Case Study 1.

FADE IN:

EXT. OSBOURNE GARDENS, A TOWN IN ENGLAND -- MORNING

Osbourne Gardens is a street of two-storey terraced
houses in the middle of a typical working class
estate somewhere in England. Each house has a small
garden at the front; a pebble dashed exterior,
slate roof and slightly larger back garden. The
houses show their age and high level of benefit
dependency in the area.

It's a hot, sunny morning in June around eleven
o'clock.

The front door of number thirteen opens and an old
man steps out to collect a bottle of milk from the
doorstep.

MAXWELL 'MAX' MONTGOMERY is in his late sixties,
of average height and slim build. Despite his age
he still sports a good head of dark hair, which he
combs well back. He wears glasses, an old cardigan
and trousers. Max, like his house, is as neat and
well kept as his age and pension allows. He lives
alone. His wife died two years earlier.

Max pulls the morning paper from the letterbox and
folds it under his arm. He scans the street for a
moment then disappears back indoors.

INT. THE KITCHEN, MAX'S HOUSE -- MOMENTS LATER

Max sets the milk and paper down on the table
beside his half eaten breakfast and a pot of tea.

A framed photo of his dead wife stands on the worktop
beside an old portable television. Nearby, another
old photo. Max and some old army buddies pose with
their rifles in a jungle clearing somewhere in Borneo.

                              MAX
                    (to wife's picture)
                 Morning, Tess.

He straightens it then smiles.

                              MAX
                 I know, I know, don't forget
                 your pills.

He opens some tablet boxes and takes out an
assortment of multi-coloured pills and capsules,
his heart medication.

He pours a glass of water and swallows the first
tablet. As he sips a door bangs next door in
number eleven.

A male voice shouts abuse.

Max sets his glass down and walks into the hallway.

THE HALLWAY

Max cocks an ear towards the adjoining wall.

All is quiet.

Just the Baxters at it again.

After a few moments Max shrugs and returns to the
kitchen.

THE KITCHEN

Max completely forgets his medication and turns on the
radio. A Radio presenter moans about reality TV shows.

Max clears his breakfast plate, checks the heat of
the teapot then pours himself a fresh cup of tea.

He browses a few pages of his newspaper then stops to butter a piece of cold toast. Satisfied, he munches toast and reads.

After a few moments a door bangs hard again next door.

More raised voices.

The male voice yells something that Max can't quite make out. He stops, listens, but then goes on reading.

He only gets a few lines further down the page before the row escalates. The male voice is the loudest but now Max can hear a woman's voice as well as a young child crying. The words are too muffled to decipher.

Max gets up, turns off the radio and listens.

The voices rise and fall with the ebb and flow of the argument.

Max lifts an empty glass and enters the hallway again.

THE HALLWAY

Max places the glass against the wall and puts his ear to it.

INT. BAXTER'S LIVING ROOM -- CONTINUOUS

RALF BAXTER, late twenties, shaven headed, face contorted with rage, holds a white sports top inches from the face of his terrified wife, JANICE.

                    RALF
          You call that washed, do you?
          Do you? Look at it!

Janice, tears flowing, doesn't reply. She has a red mark on her face as well as an old bruise below her right eye.

Their two little children, eight-year-old LIAM and six-year-old ALICE stand shaking by the door to the kitchen. Alice cries for her mother.

> RALF
>
> Look at it, you stupid bitch!
> Does that look fucking clean?
> Does it!

> JANICE
>
> No... I'm sorry.

> RALF
>
> Sorry! Sorry! I'm sorry...
> sorry I ever married you, you
> useless piece of shite.

He catches sight of Alice crying, and screams at her too.

> RALF
>
> And what the fuck are you
> yamming about? Shut up, SHUT
> UP. You're useless, just like
> your Ma. Fuck up!

Alice, terrified, cries even more. Liam tries to shield his little sister. He holds her tight in his arms but Ralf grabs her from him with both hands.

> RALF
>
> You want your ma? There she
> is then.

He flings Alice bodily across the room to land on the floor at her mother's feet. Alice cries out with pain and terror.

                    RALF
          There's your brat.

Janice reacts at once.

                    JANICE
          Leave her alone, she's only a
          child.

She clasps Alice to her.

                    JANICE
          Don't you dare touch her.

                    RALF
          Or you'll do what? Eh! You'll
          do fucking what!

                    JANICE
          Oh yeah, you're a big man
          now, hitting a little child.

Ralf slaps Janice on the face.

The kids scream but it only seems to antagonise
him. He slaps Janice repeatedly. She recoils from
his blows, grabs Alice and retreats through the
kitchen towards the back door.

Liam cuts across and tries to block his father.

                    LIAM
          Mum!
                    (tries to hold his
                    father back)
          Daddy stop, please stop!

Ralf pushes him out of the way. There's a crazed
glint in his eye. Janice screams at him.

> JANICE
> Leave him alone! If you touch
> them again, I'm going to the
> police. You hear me?

> RALF
> Go on then, you do that, you
> fucking bitch, do it and
> you'll never see them again,
> you hear me.

Janice runs out the back door into the garden with
Alice in her arms.

INT. THE HALLWAY, MAX'S HOUSE -- CONTINUOUS

Max sighs. His eyes say it all.

Now the angry voices echo through Max's open
kitchen window.

He hurries into the kitchen.

INT. THE KITCHEN, MAX'S HOUSE -- CONTINUOUS

Max crosses to the window.

> JANICE (O.S.)
> (from next door)
> Don't touch him! Leave him
> alone! LEAVE HIM ALONE!

Max leans across the worktop and stretches on tip
toes to see out his kitchen window.

> RALF (O.S.)
> Go on then get the cops, you
> think I'm fucking scared, get
> them, it'll be the last thing
> you do!

The children cry.

> LIAM (O.S.)
> Daddy, daddy, please, stop
> hurting Mummy.

Max stretches up as far as he can but it's no good
he can't see. There's a sound like a bin being
knocked over and scuffling. Max heads for the stairs.

THE STAIRS

He runs up the stairs as fast as he can, panting as
he climbs. At the top he's flushed and breathless.

He rushes into the back bedroom, his own bedroom.

INT. THE BACK BEDROOM, MAX'S HOUSE -- CONTINUOUS

Max pulls aside the net curtains to look down into
the Baxters' garden.

EXT. BAXTERS' BACK GARDEN -- CONTINUOUS

Ralf and Janice scuffle.

The children pull at their arms and cry for them to
stop.

Just then, Ralf grabs Janice by the hair. She
screams as he drags her bodily back inside the
kitchen.

The children follow.

The back door slams.

The angry voices fade in intensity.

INT. THE BACK BEDROOM, MAX'S HOUSE -- CONTINUOUS

Max lets go of the curtain and steps back but just as he does so he catches sight of a girl sunbathing in the back garden of number fifteen - the Taylors'.

A sharp intake of breath.

He steps to one side then, thinking he won't be seen, peeps around the edge of the net curtain.

EXT. TAYLORS' BACK GARDEN -- MOMENTS LATER

Samantha 'Sam' Taylor sunbathes on a deck chair type sun lounger.

She's heard the Baxters fighting but shows no interest. She's more interested in the curtain movement she's noticed at Max's bedroom window.

Samantha Taylor is a precocious, sexually aware seventeen year old with a reputation for exhibitionism and a body to die for. Sam knows the power of her body and knows how to use it. Playing Lolita is one of her favourite pastimes. Now she's noticed Max.

Looking up through her designer sunglasses she can just make him out hiding in the shadows at the edge of his bedroom window.

She smiles to herself, a knowing little smile, then picks up the lollipop she's been sucking and licks it suggestively like the girls she's seen in porno DVDs at parties. She licks her finger.

Sam, already nicely tanned, wears a skimpy red bikini with a sheer wrap around her waist and legs. She stretches and opens her legs so the wrap falls open exposing her thighs.

She lifts a bottle of suntan oil from the ground
beside her, squeezes some onto her hands then
sensuously massages the oil into her upper arms and
body.

She slides her hands inside the top of her bikini
massaging each of her breasts in turn. She gives a
coy smile and glances up at Max's window.

INT. THE BACK BEDROOM, MAX'S HOUSE -- CONTINUOUS

Max stands mesmerised, silently watching.

He can't take his eyes off Sam.

Max's heart thumps with excitement. His breathing
becomes laboured. A little vein pulses in his neck.

The Baxters can still be heard arguing in the
background but Max barely notices.

EXT. TAYLORS' BACK GARDEN -- MOMENTS LATER

Sam massages oil on her stomach and abdomen.

Just then Sam's mother opens the back door and
calls to her. Sam replies with the voice of a
little girl, the picture of innocence.

> SAM'S MOTHER
>
> Sam.

> SAM
>
> Yes.

> SAM'S MOTHER
> I'm away down town. I'll be
> back in an hour or two.

                          SAM

        Okay.

                     SAM'S MOTHER
        Don't be lying out there
        all day, you'll get burnt,
        and for God's sake put some
        clothes on.

                          SAM
        Okay, Mum, just another half
        hour.

                     SAM'S MOTHER
        Right, I'm away then. D'you
        want anything back?

                          SAM
        No.

                     SAM'S MOTHER
        Okay, see you later then.

                          SAM
        Bye.

The back door closes.

Sam stretches back and looks up at Max's window.
Her body glistens in the sunlight. She's pleased to
see his shadow is still there.

She hears the front door of her own house slam then
smiles.

She reaches up and very deliberately unties her
bikini top and sets it to one side, topless.

INT. THE BACK BEDROOM, MAX'S HOUSE -- CONTINUOUS

A sharp intake of breath.

Max stares down at Sam's breasts.

Tense, he breathes faster.

His heart beats louder than before, thumping in his ears.

He stares down at Sam as she slowly massages oil over her breasts in a circular motion. His eyes follow every movement of her fingertips.

Sam's breasts completely fill his vision.

EXT. TAYLOR'S BACK GARDEN -- CONTINUOUS

Sam glances up in his direction as she works her body. She knows exactly what she's doing and enjoys every minute of it.

INT. THE BACK BEDROOM, MAX'S HOUSE -- CONTINUOUS

Max pulls his head back from the window as she glances up but doesn't lose sight of her.

EXT. TAYLORS' BACK GARDEN

Sam unties the wrap around her waist, lifts her hips, pulls it free and drops it to the ground.

She arches her body and stretches her arms back over her head striking a pose like a Playboy centrefold.

INT. THE BACK BEDROOM, MAX'S HOUSE -- CONTINUOUS

Transfixed, Max is barely able to hide his presence at the window anymore.

He holds the edge of the curtain slightly open.

Heart thumping, he hears a ringing in his ears.

EXT. TAYLORS' BACK GARDEN -- CONTINUOUS

Sam sighs with contentment and holds her Playboy
centrefold pose as she basks in the sun. She
watches Max's curtain move, squinting through her
sunglasses.

Suddenly there's a crash and loud burst of sound as
the Baxter's back door bursts open again.

Sam jumps with fright, then looks up over the
wooden fence that separates her garden and Max's.

EXT. BAXTERS' BACK GARDEN -- CONTINUOUS

A violent commotion.

Ralf and Janice spill out into the garden again.

INT. THE BACK BEDROOM, MAX'S HOUSE -- CONTINUOUS

Max also jumps at the sudden noise and turns to
look down into the Baxters' garden.

His heart beats loudly with shock, a vein pulses in
his neck.

He steps forward to the window to look no longer
caring whether Sam can see him or not.

EXT. BAXTERS' BACK GARDEN -- CONTINUOUS

Janice backs into the corner of the garden holding
Alice in front of her. She holds a deadly looking
kitchen knife in her right hand and points it at
Ralf.

She's hysterical now, frightened beyond belief.

>   JANICE
>   If you touch her again I'll
>   stab you, I mean it, d'you
>   hear me? Never again!

She holds the boning knife high in front of her and waves the tip of it at Ralf.

Mad with rage, Ralf strikes a macho pose and edges towards her with his arms and hands held out wide. He exposes his chest and taunts her, challenging her to strike. He beckons with his open hands and goads her.

>   RALF
>   Come on then! Do it, do it
>   you fucking bitch!

Liam tries to block him again.

>   LIAM
>   Daddy! Please stop. Don't
>   hurt Mummy!

Ralf swipes him aside and knocks him to the ground.

Suddenly he lunges at Janice and grapples with her. For several moments they wrestle, fighting for the knife.

The children scream.

Ralf jumps back. Now, he has the knife.

Janice cries out, there's blood running down her arm and stomach. She's been stabbed. She slumps to a sitting position on the ground with Alice hanging on to her. The colour drains from her face as she looks down at her side in disbelief.

                    JANICE
          My God. My God.

                    ALICE
          Mummy! Mummy! You're
          bleeding!

                    JANICE
               (half to herself)
          I don't want my kids to die.
          I don't want my...
               (aloud)
          Help me someone! He's going to
          kill us, please God help me!

Ralf doesn't appear to hear her and continues his
macho posing with a crazed expression on his face.
He looks like he's high on drugs.

                    RALF
          You want more, eh? Do you, do
          you?

He laughs madly.

                    RALF
          Who's going to the cops now?
          Eh?

                    JANICE
               (weak)
          Ralf, please, no more, don't
          hurt the children, please
          Ralf... please...

                    RALF
          You see what happens if you
          fuck with me. Go to the cops
          and you'll never see them
          alive again!

Suddenly he grabs Liam in front of him and holds
the razor sharp boning knife right under his
throat. The boy screams in terror.

INT. THE BACK BEDROOM, MAX'S HOUSE -- CONTINUOUS

Max is horrified.

Sound of his heart beating.

In a panic, he pulls open his wardrobe and
rummages through the top shelves. Clothes scatter
everywhere. An old cardboard shoebox topples to the
floor. Old army medals, tunic badges, photos and
faded letters spill out.

Outside, the yelling continues. Unintelligible,
other voices join in. Max can hear the Baxters
screaming.

>   ALICE (O.S.)
>   Mummy! Mummy! Someone help my
>   mummy!

Max's heart beats louder and louder.

>   JANICE (O.S.)
>   Liam! Oh God, No, Ralf, No!

>   LIAM (O.S.)
>   Mummy!

Max pulls out the top drawer of his chest of
drawers. A bit too far, it upends and falls to the
floor spilling its contents. Among them, a small
cardboard ammo box, many years old. It splits open
on impact and scatters two dozen .38 revolver
bullets across the floor. Frantically, Max searches
through the mound of clothes until finally he finds
it.

He unwraps an old shirt and there in the middle of it - a World War Two era army issue .38 revolver. A souvenir.

He breaks it open then falls to his knees desperately searching for the bullets. Hands shaking he loads its cylindrical chamber with six rounds. He snaps it shut then pulls himself up using one hand on the side of the chest of drawers.

Thumping heart beats.

He looks pale, flustered.

He rushes out of the bedroom, stumbles down the stairs and runs out into his own back garden.

EXT. MAX'S BACK GARDEN -- CONTINUOUS

Aware of noise all around him Max runs down the path to his back gate.

Out of the corner of his eye he can see Ralf still holding the knife to Liam's throat and the bright red blood on Janice's clothes.

Drawn by the shouting, other neighbours have come out and are looking over their fences trying to see what's going on. Some are shouting at Ralf to stop but it's all a blur to Max.

Heart beat thumping.

He reaches the gate and tugs the bolt open. He runs through the laneway to the Baxters' back garden gate. He fumbles for the lock but it is already open.

The gate swings wide.

He rushes in.

Pandemonium.

EXT. BAXTERS' BACK GARDEN -- CONTINUOUS

As he walks in he catches sight of Janice. She
looks pale, in shock and mutters to herself.

> JANICE
> Please God, don't let my kids
> die.

She sees Max, so does Ralf.

With shaven head Ralf looks mean. He wears a tight
white body builder's top to show off his muscles
and chest. His forearms are tattooed and he has a
crazed look in his eye.

Hands shaking, Max raises his revolver and points
it at Ralf's chest.

> MAX
> Stop! Let him go!
> (Ralf laughs)
> I'll shoot! I will!

> RALF
> Go on then, Granddad, give it
> your best shot.

Ralf raises the knife closer to Liam's throat.
Brimming with aggression and rage he screams at Max.

> RALF
> Go ahead then you old
> bastard. Go on, you old fart,
> do it! DO IT! DO IT!

He bares his chest to Max.

                    MAX
          I will, I will... if you
          don't let the boy go.

Max trembles.

His aim wavers.

Janice screams and begs Ralf.

                    JANICE
          Ralf! Please, Ralf, don't
          hurt him. Please don't hurt
          him.
               (to Max)
          Please don't let him hurt my
          little boy.

Janice, white faced and badly blood stained now
looks faint. Alice holds her wounded mother as she
sits on the ground.

Ralf just laughs.

Heart beat thumping.

                    MAX
          Let him go!

Ralf becomes even more aggressive.

                    RALF
          Who the fuck do you think you
          are? Get the fuck out of my
          garden!

                    MAX
          Let him go! I'll use it, I
          promise you, I'll use it. Let
          him go!

Max's hand shakes so much the tip of the revolver barrel waves wildly all over the place. He tries to steady it, to keep it aimed at Ralf's chest but he feels a little dizzy.

Heart beat thumping.

His nerves on edge, Max is white with fear.

Other voices sound all around him.

> NEIGHBOUR #1
> Someone get the police.

> NEIGHBOUR #2
> Watch out! He's got a gun.

> NEIGHBOUR #3
> Max, don't do it, you're only
> making him worse. Leave it to
> the police.

> NEIGHBOUR #1
> My God, Janice's bleeding...

> NEIGHBOUR #2
> He stabbed her!

> NEIGHBOUR #1
> Someone get an ambulance.

Max looks nervously from left to right and back to Ralf and the boy. He's scared, not sure what to do.

Ralf taunts him.

> RALF
> Who do you think you are?
> Dad's army? Eh? Fuck off,
> Granddad. Get out of my
> garden!

                    JANICE
             (to Max)
          Don't let him hurt my son.
             (to Ralf)
          Ralf, for God's sake, look
          at him, he's your own son!
          Look at his face. What're you
          doing?

Someone screams and startles Max. He looks around.

To his right Sam leans on her fence. She looks
frightened. Incongruously, she's still topless and
her breasts appear to be sitting supported by the top
of her fence. Behind her Max can see other neighbours
watching. One leans out of an upstairs window.

Max looks left. More neighbours watch from their
back gardens. A little four-year-old girl looks up
at him impassively from the next garden. Suddenly,
bizarrely, she sticks her tongue out at him.

Ralf waves the knife under Liam's chin.

                    RALF
          If you don't get out now I'll
          use it!

                    LIAM
          Mummy!

Heart beat thumping, Max's tries to keep the
revolver steady.

                    MAX
          Let him go. Please, Ralf. Drop
          the knife and let him go!

Ralf suddenly becomes more aggressive and edges
forward towards Max holding the little boy at
knifepoint in front of him. Max backs away.

>   RALF
>   (teeth clenched)
>   She's never going to take my
>   kids away from me! Do you
>   understand! I'll take them
>   first!

Ralf brings the knife point right up to Liam's throat.

Janice and Alice scream.

Other people scream.

A shot.

A splash of blood hits the wall of the house right behind Ralf.

All the noise and screams abruptly cut short.

Silence.

A look of shocked disbelief on Ralf's face.

A look of disbelief on Max's face.

Slowly, he lowers the smoking revolver.

Ralf looks down at the little hole in the middle of his chest.

Suddenly blood wells up through it.

He drops the knife and clutches at the hole in his chest.

He rips and claws at his T-shirt with both hands then suddenly, his eyes roll, and he drops to the ground. Dead.

Liam throws himself across his dead father.

                    LIAM
          Daddy!

As Liam screams and hugs his father a pool of blood
begins to spread out from under his back.

Stunned, Janice and Alice join in.

                    JANICE
          Ralf! RALF! Oh my God! Oh my
          God! No! Oh, Ralf! Ralf! Dear
          God, No!

                    ALICE
          Daddy! Daddy!

Alice joins Liam hugging her father's body as
Janice drags herself across to join them.

In an instant all has changed.

Max, horrified and dazed, backs away. He looks around
to see his shocked neighbours cowering from him.

                    MAX
               (pleads)
          He was going to do it.

Those nearest him look ashen faced.

                    MAX
               (louder)
          He was going to do it.

Heart thumping, a sudden pain like an express train
slams into his chest.

Max drops the revolver and clutches at his heart.

                            MAX
                        (whispered)
                    My pills.

Heart beat thumping loud in his ears he staggers out
of the Baxters' garden, through the laneway and into
his own garden. He leans to his left as he moves.

The Baxters' wailing rings in his ears.

Breathing heavily, he struggles up the garden path
towards his kitchen. Face white, eyes closed in
pain, he gasps.

                            MAX
                No, oh no, no, no... not now.

Heartbeat thumping... drowns out all other sound.

Sam watches with a look of horror as he passes. She
backs away from the fence and covers her breasts
with her wrap.

Max half collapses half stumbles through his back
door and into the kitchen.

INT. THE KITCHEN, MAX'S HOUSE -- CONTINUOUS

Heart beat thumping. Laboured breath. Gasping.

He staggers across to the worktop and desperately
tries to open the pill boxes. He can't raise his
left arm up high enough to help. His breakfast
plates and radio crash to the floor.

Grey faced, in great pain, he claws at the worktop
trying to hold himself up. He looks at his wife's
photo.

Suddenly the sound of his heart stops mid beat.

Max gasps, twists his face and grabs for his wife's picture.

He falls backwards to the kitchen floor with his wife's picture held firmly in his right hand. He clutches her picture tight to his chest and groans in agony for a moment then everything stops.

Silence.

In the background, faint, the sound of the Baxters' crying.

Like a beach ball deflating a final breath slowly escapes from his mouth.

His right arm flops to the ground.

His wife's picture slides from his chest and clatters to the floor.

FADE OUT:

APPENDIX B

Short Screenplay:

The Door

By

Juanita Wilson

NOMINEE

82nd Academy Awards in 2009, Best Live Action Short Film

WINNER

Irish Film and Television Award – IFTA – Best Irish Short Film 2008
Best Irish Short Film – Foyle Film Festival 2008
Best First Short Film Award – Cork International Film Festival 2008
Gold Medal – Bilbao International Film Festival 2008
Best Director – World OFF Film Awards, Warsaw, Poland 2009
Katrin Cartlidge Bursary – Sarajevo Film Festival 2009

Note: As far as possible original formatting has been preserved with only minor adjustments to meet the needs of publication in book format. The original page numbers have been dropped as in this published format the page length is slightly different. The original version was exactly five pages long. This is the original screenplay – the final film contains some minor differences in terms of dialogue delivery. This screenplay should be read in conjunction with the chapter entitled Case Study 2.

FADE IN.

The sound of WIND BLOWING over black.

EXT. APARTMENT BLOCK -- NIGHT

The wind blows through a large, half derelict apartment building.

In the darkness, a dishevelled figure drifts through the shadows, he could be a ragged ghost, or a lithe burglar. He breathes fast, anxious.

He reaches the heavy wooden front door of an apartment and lets himself in.

INT. APARTMENT -- NIGHT

The figure, NIKOLAI, a young man, his face older than his years, stands transfixed in the apartment, waiting for his eyes to adjust to the darkness. He takes in the modest domestic scene, the table set for dinner, family photos on the wall, a small pair of boots on the mat by the door.

He takes a large chisel from his pocket and sets to work on the hinges of the heavy wooden door. His

strokes are firm, strong, determination in his face.
A few attempts, then success. With a heavy CREAK,
the door swings down, pivoting on its lower hinges.

> GUARD (O.S.)
> (through a
> loudspeaker)
> Halt! Stop! We'll shoot!

NIKOLAI freezes. He holds the door shut, tries to
duck down.

Through the cracked window, the beam of a torch
cuts through the darkness, illuminating the photo
of a young girl on the wall. Nikolai shrinks back
further.

> GUARD (O.S.)
> Come out and show yourself or
> I'll shoot!

Nikolai breathes heavily. Considers what to do.

Suddenly, the window smashes and glass shards
scatter everywhere. The Guard peers in through the
broken windowpane, tries to shine his torch but
can't see Nikolai cowering behind the door.

After a moment, the guard moves on leaving Nikolai
in darkness once again. He sits back and sighs with
relief.

EXT. FOREST -- NIGHT

The door is strapped to the back of a motorcycle,
which Nikolai drives through the forest at speed.
The engine of the bike screams as it labours under
the weight.

Shadows step out from the forest and watch him
drive on towards the dawn.

                    NIKOLAI (V.O.)
              That day, we didn't just lose a
              town, we lost our whole lives.
              We left on the third day.

The light bleaches out his image.

INT. APARTMENT -- DAY

Nikolai struggles to squeeze a large cat into a
suitcase but the cat hisses, runs over to LENA, his
six-year-old daughter who picks it up and pets it.

                         LENA
              Misha doesn't want to be
              squashed in a suitcase.

                       NIKOLAI
              Then we'll have to leave her.

Lena looks up at him in shock and disbelief.

ANYA, Nikolai's young wife packs up their
belongings, picking things up, putting them down
again, unsure what to take. The radio plays in the
background.

                    RADIO ANNOUNCER (V.O.)
              Do not take any belongings...
              leave everything where it
              is... it is an offence
              to remove any property
              whatsoever...

Anya glances at Nikolai anxiously. Nikolai kicks
the radio, which smashes on the floor, sending the
cat scurrying. Lena runs out after it.

                         LENA
              Misha! Misha come back!

> NIKOLAI
> Lena - leave it! Come on!

Nikolai grabs the reluctant Lena and tries to drag
her out of the apartment.

> LENA
> Misha! We're not leaving
> Misha!

> NIKOLAI
> I'll come back for her later.

Lena looks at him with her wide blue eyes.

> NIKOLAI
> I will.

He takes her hand and leads her out, followed
by the reluctant Anya. The door is slammed shut
leaving the cat alone in the gloom.

EXT. TOWN -- DAY

Nikolai, Anya and Lena join a stream of people,
laden down with bags, all walking away from the
apartment building. Fine flakes fall gently through
the air.

EXT. SNOWY LANDSCAPE -- DAY

In the far distance, a black train cuts the white
snowy landscape in half, like a pencil drawing a
line on a sheet of paper.

> NIKOLAI (V.O.)
> Little did we know that
> everything we smuggled out
> with us was a time bomb,
> slowly ticking. That we had
> become time bombs.

INT. NEW APARTMENT - KITCHEN -- DAY

In a small, cramped apartment, Anya tries to cook
dinner while another family are eating at the
table. Lena sits on the floor, drawing. The door
opens and Nikolai comes in. Lena looks up at him.

                    LENA
          Dada, when can we go home?

Nikolai frowns, glances at the old woman at the
table.

                    NIKOLAI
          This is our home now.

                    LENA
          But you said -

He goes into the bedroom. Lena glares at the other
family, gets up and follows Nikolai into the bedroom.

INT. NEW APARTMENT - BEDROOM -- NIGHT

Nikolai sits on the bed in the cramped bedroom, his
head in his hands. Lena comes in and startles him.
He reaches out and takes her hand.

                    NIKOLAI
          We are the lucky ones, Lena.
          Come.

He starts to undress her and pulls her long white
nightdress over her.

                    LENA
          When will you get Misha?

                    NIKOLAI
          Soon my darling, soon.

Suddenly he notices a large black spot on her fair, freckled arm. He looks at it anxiously, tries to hide his fear but she has already noticed it.

> LENA
> I'm not going to die dada,
> I'm still little.

He settles her in the double bed, then leans down and kisses her.

> NIKOLAI
> You'll always be my angel.

He kisses her tenderly and settles her down to sleep. She closes her eyes. As he looks at her, his eyes fill with anxiety again. He quickly switches off the bedside light.

INT. HOSPITAL -- DAY

Black boots scrape along a white floor. Skinny, pale legs stick up from the boots. Nikolai and Anya hold Lena's hands as they walk up the long white corridor of a pristine hospital.

Seven little bald girls sit on a bench waiting. They turn their heads in unison to look at the others as they pass.

Nikolai and Anya share an anxious look. Lena walks on ahead, oblivious.

INT. DOCTOR'S SURGERY -- DAY

The doctor examines the large black spot on Lena's arm. Anya looks out the window. Nikolai sits staring at the floor.

INT. NEW APARTMENT -- NIGHT

Nikolai comes into the makeshift kitchen, starts
to take off his boots. Anya is washing blood from
sheets in the sink. She turns to him.

> ANYA
> It'd be better for her to die
> than to suffer like this.

Nikolai turns away, doesn't want to hear. Anya
squeezes the cloth tight, water spatters into the
sink.

> ANYA
> Or for me to die so that I
> don't have to watch any more.

Nikolai has no answer for her.

INT. WORKSHOP -- NIGHT

By the gloomy light of a naked light bulb, Nikolai
rubs the intricately carved wooden door. He tidies
up some of the decorative carving with a sharp
knife. His face is full of pain. He works to keep
himself busy.

The first traces of light appear through the window.

> RELIGIOUS LEADER (O.S.)
> I am the light of the World.
> Anyone who follows me will
> not be walking in the dark...

EXT. APARTMENT -- DAY

From above we see Lena lying on her back with her eyes
closed. Her head is bald. She has her arms crossed on
her chest and some beads between her fingers.

She is lying on the old wooden door.

The door is being carried by six men who walk away towards the cemetery.

> NIKOLAI (V.O.)
> We put her on the door, the
> door that my father was
> laid out on, the door that
> I had to steal from my own
> apartment.

Nikolai and Anya follow the funeral procession, Nikolai reaches out and takes Anya's hand, holds it tight.

> NIKOLAI(V.O.)
> We didn't just lose a town,
> we lost our whole world.

The small procession makes its way through the snow, away into the distance, as the wind starts to blow and, here and there, snowflakes drift gently to the ground.

FADE TO BLACK.

APPENDIX C

Short Screenplay:

The Crush

By

Michael Creagh

NOMINEE

83rd Academy Awards in 2011, Best Live Action Short Film

WINNER

Best Irish Short Film – 2009 Foyle Film Festival
Special Jury Mention – 2010 Tribeca Film Festival, New York

Note: As far as possible original formatting has been preserved with only minor adjustments to meet the needs of publication in book format. The original page numbers have been dropped as in this published

format the page length is slightly different. The original version was
15 pages long. This screenplay should be read in conjunction with the
interview chapter entitled Case Study 3. Screenplay reproduced with
kind permission of Michael Creagh and Purdy Pictures.

FADE IN:

INT. CLASSROOM -- DAY

Four rows of small desks are occupied by the eight-
year-olds that make up 2A. Twenty bored little
faces look towards the blackboard where MISS PURDY
is writing tonight's homework.

> MISS PURDY
> I want you to look for the
> words Reveal, Pretend, and
> Love in your readers tonight.
> I want you to be able to
> spell them on Monday.

2A groan. The exception is ARDAL TRAVIS, who is
watching Miss Purdy and smiling.

> MISS PURDY
> Oh... so grumpy! Tell you
> what, if everyone does well
> on their spellings we might
> have a DVD next week.

2A whoop with delight. Ardal remains composed. He
discreetly opens his pencil case. Inside among the
pencils and sharpeners is a ring. It looks like
gold but close up we realise it is plastic with a
plastic ruby in its centre. Ardal takes the ring
out, places it in the palm of his hand and encloses

his fingers around it. He looks up at Miss Purdy.
The bell RINGS.

2A stampede out of the room. Ardal remains.

Miss Purdy looks at him.

> MISS PURDY
> You okay, Ardal?

Ardal rises to his feet and slow marches up to Miss
Purdy's desk. He pats his hair back. Miss Purdy
smiles. Ardal stands inches from her and takes a
deep breath. He places the shiny trinket on her
desk.

> MISS PURDY
> Oh, Ardal. It's lovely.

> ARDAL
> I used a week's pocket money.

> MISS PURDY
> Oh wow. That's far too much.
> You didn't have to...

> ARDAL
> I did. It's important that
> you know how I feel about
> you.

Miss Purdy beams.

> MISS PURDY
> Well. This is very special
> and I'll treasure it always.

Ardal smiles.

> MISS PURDY
> Does this mean we're engaged?

Ardal seems surprised.

                    ARDAL
          Well, I hadn't thought
          about it. If you want to. I
          suppose.

                  MISS PURDY
          Well, that's very sweet and
          I'll certainly give it some
          thought.

She kisses Ardal on the fringe. Now he beams.

                  MISS PURDY
          You've a good weekend, okay?

                  ARDAL
          Yes, Miss. I definitely will.

EXT. PLAYING FIELDS -- DAY

Ardal is walking home with that same smile on his
face.

INT. KITCHEN -- NIGHT

Ardal is sitting having dinner with his mum and
dad. Dad wears a blue Garda (Irish police) shirt.

                  DAD
          So how was everyone's day?

                  MUM
          You're hoarse.

                  DAD
          Screaming at some kid with a
          crossbow.

                  MUM
          No.

                    DAD
          Yeah. Wee shite was off his
          head on glue and trying
          to rob a newsagents. Had
          the go-ahead to shoot and
          everything.

                   ARDAL
          Oh, cool. Did you waste him?

                    MUM
          Eh. It's not cool, Ardal. No
          more Cowboy films.

                    DAD
              (laughing)
          No. He backed down in the
          end, thank God. Otherwise I'd
          be sitting here with an arrow
          in me head.

Dad pretends his fork is in his eye. Ardal giggles.

                    MUM
              (shakes head)
          Where are these kids' parents?

                   ARDAL
          Mum, what age can a person
          get married at?

Mum and Dad smile at each other.

                    MUM
          I think it's sixteen. Why?
          Have you got some news for
          us?

                   ARDAL
          No. Well. Not yet. I'll keep
          you posted.

INT. ARDAL'S ROOM -- NIGHT

Ardal's room is small and dominated by a huge
poster of two duelling cowboys. Ardal leafs through
a multiyear diary. He arrives at May 30, 2015. He
writes "Marry Miss Purdy".

INT. SHOPPING MALL -- DAY

Ardal is lagging several metres behind his mum.

>   MUM
>   Come on, Ardal. You're
>   dawdling!

Miss Purdy comes out of a nearby jeweller shop.
Ardal is taken aback.

>   MISS PURDY
>   Hello, Ardal. Bought anything
>   nice?

>   ARDAL
>   Boots.

Ardal points to his gleaming footwear.

>   MISS PURDY
>   Oh, lovely. They make you
>   look very smart.

>   ARDAL
>   They're cowboy boots.

He pulls up his trouser leg to show.

>   MISS PURDY
>   Wow. Very cool.

Ardal smiles.

>   MISS PURDY
>   I got something special
>   myself.

She holds out her hand. Ardal's mum has approached.

>   MUM
>   Hello, Miss Purdy. Oh my
>   goodness! Someone's a lucky
>   girl. That's gorgeous.

On Miss Purdy's finger is a sizeable diamond ring.
Ardal's face falls slightly.

>   MISS PURDY
>   Thanks, Mrs Travis.

Miss Purdy's BOYFRIEND has just come out of the
jewellers. He's fiddling with his wallet. Ardal's
expression shifts from disappointment to a dark,
Kubrickian rage.

>   MISS PURDY
>   This is my boy... Oh, I
>   mean my fiancé, Pierce. This
>   is Ardal, one of my second
>   classers… and his mum.

>   MUM
>   (to boyfriend)
>   Congratulations.

>   BOYFRIEND
>   Yeah. Cheers. Kat, are we
>   done here yet? The match is
>   starting in ten minutes.

>   MISS PURDY
>   I thought we'd get a
>   celebratory lunch.

                         BOYFRIEND
                I think you've fleeced me
                enough today as it is. C'mon,
                I don't want to miss kick off.

He gives her a little shove in the arm. Ardal
notices this.

                         MISS PURDY
                Ok. Bye, Ardal. Bye, Mrs Travis.

Ardal does not answer. The couple leave.

INT. ARDAL'S ROOM -- NIGHT

Ardal rips out May 30, 2015. He stares at it for a
moment. He throws it to the ground and stamps on
it. He looks down at his new cowboy boots and then
up at the poster.

INT. LANDING -- NIGHT

Through a half open door Ardal can see his dad,
shirt off, handling a black handgun. He places it on
a high shelf in his wardrobe.

Ardal watches intently. Then he goes to his room.

INT. ARDAL'S ROOM

Ardal picks the crumpled diary page up from the
floor. He looks up at his poster. He places the page
back in his diary.

INT. CLASSROOM -- DAY

The bell rings.

                         MISS PURDY
                Now, remember your spellings,
                please!

The children file out.

                    MISS PURDY
             Hey, Ardal.

Ardal looks at Miss Purdy darkly and walks on.

                    MISS PURDY
             Ardal Travis. Come here,
             please.

Ardal obeys sullenly.

                    MISS PURDY
             What's up, Ardal?

                    ARDAL
             I see you're wearing his ring
             and not mine.

                    MISS PURDY
             Oh.

Miss Purdy blushes slightly.

                    MISS PURDY
             It's complicated, Ardal.
             Someday you'll…

                    ARDAL
              How's it complicated? He's no
             good for you, Miss.

Miss Purdy sniggers.

                    MISS PURDY
             Sorry, pet. Go on.

                    ARDAL
              It's all right. You'll see
             anyway.

                          MISS PURDY
                What do you mean?

                            ARDAL
                Nothing. You'll just see I'm
                the one that loves you.

                          MISS PURDY
                Ach, Ardal. I know you do.
                And you're very special to me
                too. But sometimes grown-ups,
                we have to...

                            ARDAL
                I have to go home, Miss. Bye.

Ardal walks to the door. He stops and looks back at
her. She smiles warmly.

                            ARDAL
                I would have taken you for
                lunch.

                          MISS PURDY
                What?

                            ARDAL
                I would have missed the
                football and taken you to
                lunch.

Miss Purdy's smile slips a little. Ardal leaves.

INT/EXT. CAR PARK -- DAY

Miss Purdy's boyfriend is sitting in his car
drumming on the steering wheel.

                          BOYFRIEND
                Come on, wom-an. Always the
                friggin' last.

He jumps at a TAP on the window. Ardal is staring
in at him. He winds it down.

> BOYFRIEND
> Well hello there. And what
> can I do for you?

> ARDAL
> Don't marry Miss Purdy.

> BOYFRIEND
> Come again?

> ARDAL
> I'm telling you you're not to
> marry Miss Purdy.

> BOYFRIEND
> And why's that then?

> ARDAL
> Because she's mine.

The boyfriend starts to laugh.

> BOYFRIEND
> Well. That is a dilemma.

> ARDAL
> Don't laugh at me.

> BOYFRIEND
> Sorry, pal. But you know...
> All's fair in love and war.
> See, she told me you were
> just too short.

> ARDAL
> She never said that.

                          BOYFRIEND
              Yeah… And that you weren't
              financially stable enough to
              cater for her needs. She's
              a high maintenance lady you
              know.

                            ARDAL
              I don't know what that means.

                          BOYFRIEND
              Oh, you will mate. You will.

                            ARDAL
              You talk stupid.

                          BOYFRIEND
              Ah now. Don't be gettin'
              all...

                            ARDAL
              Meet me in a duel.

                          BOYFRIEND
                  A what?

                            ARDAL
              A duel. Just you and me.
              Round in the hand-ball court.
              Tomorrow after school.

The boyfriend cannot contain his mirth and is
laughing quite openly now.

                            ARDAL
                  To the death.

The boyfriend laughs even more. He manages to
compose himself a bit.

                    BOYFRIEND
          Okay. What are we fighting
          with? Swords, pistols,
          conkers?

                    ARDAL
          Pistols.

                    BOYFRIEND
          By Jove. It's a date sir.

                    ARDAL
          See you there.

                    BOYFRIEND
          And may the best man... or
          boy win!

Ardal walks off. Miss Purdy gets into the car.

                    MISS PURDY
          What's tickled you?

                    BOYFRIEND
          Oh you got to hear this.

EXT. PLAYING FIELDS -- DAY

Ardal is walking home. His face is stern.

INT. PARENTS' BEDROOM -- NIGHT

Ardal sits on his parents' bed staring up at his
Dad's wardrobe.

EXT. CAR PARK -- DAY

The boyfriend's car is waiting for Miss Purdy.
The boyfriend again is drumming his fingers on the
wheel.

> BOYFRIEND
>
> Come on.

Miss Purdy gets into the car and kisses him. He's
about to drive off when he spots Ardal walk round
the back of the school. He turns off the ignition.

> BOYFRIEND
>
> Oh wait. I've got to see
> this.

> MISS PURDY
>
> What?

> BOYFRIEND
>
> I've an appointment with
> death remember?

> MISS PURDY
>
> Oh, leave it. Don't be mean
> to him.

> BOYFRIEND
>
> Aw, c'mon. I just want to
> see. You can stay here if you
> like.

The boyfriend leaves the car.

EXT. HANDBALL COURT -- DAY

The boyfriend looks around the court. He sees no
sign of Ardal.

He moves to leave. Ardal appears at the opening,
carrying his schoolbag.

> BOYFRIEND
>
> I was beginning to think you
> wouldn't show.

                    ARDAL
        Where's your gun?

                    BOYFRIEND
        Ah, think I've forgotten it.
        Silly me, eh?

                    ARDAL
        That's not my problem.

                    BOYFRIEND
        I suppose not. So then,
        where's your...

Ardal opens his bag and pulls out a black handgun
that looks like a cannon in his little hands.

                    BOYFRIEND
        ...gun? That's not real.

                    ARDAL
        Yes it is.

Miss Purdy arrives at the doorway of the court.

                    MISS PURDY
        What's going... Ardal! What
        are you doing?

Ardal points the handgun at boyfriend.

                    BOYFRIEND
        That's not... Now, don't
        point... That's not real.
        It's a toy. Isn't it, son?

                    ARDAL
        It's not a toy.

                    MISS PURDY
        Ardal put that down now.

                        BOYFRIEND
              Where would you get a real...

                         ARDAL
              My Dad's a Garda.

Boyfriend looks at Miss Purdy for affirmation. She nods.

                        BOYFRIEND
              Hang on. Guards aren't armed.

                         ARDAL
              The Emergency Response Unit
              are.

Boyfriend looks again at Miss Purdy. She nods again.

                        BOYFRIEND
              You couldn't have told me
              about this?

Miss Purdy shrugs nervously.

                        BOYFRIEND
              Jesus. Now be careful wee
              man. J-j-just...

                         ARDAL
              Don't marry teacher.

                        BOYFRIEND
              J-j-just put that thing down
              and we can talk about it.

                         ARDAL
              Say you won't marry Miss
              Purdy. You don't deserve her.

                        BOYFRIEND
              W-Wha... You... Why... You
              don't even know me.

                    ARDAL
        I know you're not good enough
        for her.

                    BOYFRIEND
        Why?

                    ARDAL
        Because you're a dickhead.

                    MISS PURDY
        Ardal Travis!

                    ARDAL
        Sorry, Miss.

                    BOYFRIEND
        Are you just gonna stand there
        and watch one of your second-
        classers blow my head off.

                    MISS PURDY
        He won't...

                    BOYFRIEND
        Have you not seen City of
        God? Get a fuckin' cop or
        something!

                    ARDAL
        Stay there, Miss.

                    MISS PURDY
        Ardal, please. Put it down.
        I'm going to have to put it
        on your report. What will
        your mum and dad say?

                    ARDAL
        I told you I'd show you,
        Miss.

                    BOYFRIEND
        Now, listen to your teacher,
        son.

                     ARDAL
        Tell her you won't marry her.

                    BOYFRIEND
        I'm not going to tell her
        that...

Ardal's little thumb expertly unhitches the safety.
The click is amplified by the handball court walls.

                      ARDAL
        Tell her.

                    BOYFRIEND
        Oh for fu... J-j-j-ust hold
        on there. J-j-

Ardal cocks the handgun and his finger curls around
the trigger. Boyfriend begins to cry like a child.
He lowers himself to his knees.

                    BOYFRIEND
        Okay! Okay! You can have her!
        I never wanted to marry her
        anyway!

                    MISS PURDY
             (stunned)
        Excuse me?

                    BOYFRIEND
        She moaned constantly about
        it. She did my head in. I
        thought putting a ring on her
        finger would shut her up for a
        while. I don't want to... be
        married!

There is silence. Ardal straightens his aim.

> BOYFRIEND
>> Please. Please. Ardal… Ardal?
>> Please don't shoot me.
>> Please...
>>> (to Miss Purdy)
>> Get someone you stupid bitch!

BANG!

The massive crack reverberates around the walls.
Miss Purdy screams.

Boyfriend is lying on the ground. His eyes fixed in
a petrified stare.

A little plastic orange ball rolls past his face.

He blinks.

> ARDAL
>> (to Miss Purdy)
> See, Miss.

Miss Purdy nods while looking at her prone fiancé.
Boyfriend raises himself onto his hands.

Miss Purdy pulls off her engagement ring and throws
it onto the ground in front of him.

> MISS PURDY
> You dick-head.

Boyfriend looks at Ardal. His face darkens with
malice. He makes towards the boy.

> BOYFRIEND
> You little bastard.

                    MISS PURDY
          You come anywhere near him
          and I'll tell everyone you're
          a... kiddie fiddler. Come on,
          Ardal.

EXT. PLAYING FIELDS -- DAY

Miss Purdy and Ardal are walking away from the
handball court.

                    ARDAL
          Will this go on my report,
          Miss?

                    MISS PURDY
          Maybe we'll keep this between
          ourselves. But maybe you
          should give me that for
          safekeeping.

Ardal hands her the gun.

                    MISS PURDY
          God, it's realistic. Where
          did you get it?

                    ARDAL
          My dad was hiding it in his
          wardrobe for my birthday.
          Nice, isn't it?

                    MISS PURDY
          Eh... it's certainly very
          pretty. I'll just pop it in
          here though for now.

She puts the toy gun in her bag. She removes
something else.

                  MISS PURDY
          Oh. What's this?

She pulls out Ardal's plastic ring. She slides it
onto her little finger and gives Ardal a big warm
smile.

                  ARDAL
          It's okay, Miss. I've decided
          not to marry you after all.

                  MISS PURDY
          Oh? Why's that?

                  ARDAL
          I'm not financially stable
          enough to cater for your
          needs.

Miss Purdy can't help but giggle.

                  ARDAL
          And someone as nice as you
          should have everything she
          wants.

She smiles and her eyes well.

                  MISS PURDY
          Someday some girl's going to
          be very lucky.

                  ARDAL
          Meh. Girls are stupid.

                  MISS PURDY
          Well. We certainly can be.

She puts her arm around Ardal's shoulder.

> MISS PURDY
> Come on, Romeo. I'll get you
> home.

They walk off together as the sun sets over the
football pitches.

FADE OUT.

THE END

INDEX

drama, 21–5, 42, 45–6, 48,
    53, 55–7, 59–68, 87, 98,
    102, 106–7, 118, 122,
    134, 138, 141, 146, 166,
    174–5, 185, 189–90
dread, 108, 115

E

Egri, Lajos, 97
Eight, 185
emotional experience, 10–11,
    27–8, 49, 54, 109–10,
    112–14, 117
emotional identification, 95
emotional impact, 45, 87, 111,
    116, 145, 181
emotions, 46, 53, 57, 102,
    105, 109–17, 135, 178
empathy, 95–7
end/ending, 36–7, 46, 51, 54,
    63, 66, 83, 87–90, 112–13,
    136, 141–2, 152, 168
English Patient, The, 112
Ermey, Lee, 128
excitement, 110, 113, 153
expectations, 114, 116–17,
    133
experimental, 36, 38–40
exposition, 78, 93, 125, 153,
    170, 178

F

fades, 73
false resolutions, 87

fear, 57, 98, 104, 115–17,
    127
feedback, 25, 150, 160,
    162–3, 177
festivals, 9, 16, 18, 23, 25,
    38–42, 50, 83, 119, 139,
    158–9, 164, 173
Field, Syd, 82, 181
Final Draft, 71, 187
first impressions, 83, 94, 142,
    165
flashback, 33, 73, 78
For The Birds, 37
foreign languages, 126
foreshadow, 114, 117, 120
format/formatting, 149, 187
four-minute rule, 83
Foyle Film Festival, 9–11, 18,
    35, 158, 173, 183
Franzoni, David, 58
Friedmann, Julian, 10, 145
Full Metal Jacket, 128
funding, 17, 23, 34, 41, 69,
    111, 139, 142, 144, 170

G

Gladiator, 31, 47, 141
Goldman, William, 90
Great Train Robbery, 12
Griffiths, DW, 13

H

Harris, Thomas, 58
Hauge, Michael, 110

kamera BOOKS

ESSENTIAL READING FOR ANYONE INTERESTED IN FILM AND POPULAR CULTURE

Tackling a wide range of subjects from prominent directors, popular genres and current trends through to cult films, national cinemas and film concepts and theories.

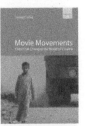
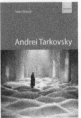

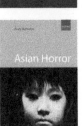

Neo-Noir
Contemporary Film Noir
From *Chinatown* to *The Dark Knight*
Douglas Keesey
978-1-84243-311-9 **£12.99**

Movie Movements
Films That Changed the World of Cinema
James Clarke
978-1-84243-305-8 **£12.99**

Andrei Tarkovsky
Sean Martin
978-1-84243-366-9 **£16.99**

John Carpenter
Michelle Le Blanc & Colin Odell
978-1-84243-338-6 **£12.99**

Blaxploitation Films
Mikel J. Koven
978-1-84243-334-8 **£12.99**

Asian Horror
Andy Richards
978-1-84243-320-1 **£12.99**